INTEREST GROUPS IN AMERICAN CAMPAIGNS

The New Face of Electioneering

Mark J. Rozell
UNIVERSITY OF PENNSYLVANIA

Clyde Wilcox
GEORGETOWN UNIVERSITY

A Division of Congressional Quarterly Inc.
Washington, D.C.

To Renée Kathryn Rozell,
born April 12, 1998
M.J.R.

To the memory of my mother,
Sarah Louise Wilcox
C.W.

Copyright © 1999 Congressional Quarterly Inc.

Printed in the United States of America

Library of Congress Cataloging-in-Publication Data

Rozell, Mark J.
    Interest groups in American campaigns : the new face of
electioneering / Mark J. Rozell, Clyde Wilcox.
        p.   cm.
    Includes bibliographical references and index.
    ISBN 1-56802-392-8
    1. Pressure groups--United States.   2. Lobbying--United States.
3. Electioneering--United States.   4. United States--Politics and
government--20th century.   I. Wilcox, Clyde, 1953- .   II. Title.
JK1118.R7   1998
324'.4'0973--dc21   98-38324

Contents

Preface

Over the past several elections, interest groups have become increasingly active. They have endorsed candidates more often, contributed more money to candidates and parties, distributed more voters' guides, and called more citizens to encourage them to vote. They have taken on new activities as well: a number of groups collectively spent millions of dollars in 1996 to advocate issues and, indirectly, candidates. It is possible that the American electoral system is in the process of its second major transition: first our elections changed from party centered to candidate centered, and now they may focus increasingly on the agendas of coalitions of interest groups.

Although there are many excellent texts on the market that briefly cover the role of interest groups in elections, we believed that there was a need for a more comprehensive book. In this volume, we describe and analyze the wide array of strategies and tactics adopted by interest groups in U.S. national elections. Our organizing principle is that interest group electoral activity involves communication: communication with political parties, with candidates, and with voters. Thus, in Chapter 2, we discuss the ways in which groups ally themselves with parties, attempt to influence the candidates that the parties nominate, and the platforms they adopt. In Chapter 3, we focus on the methods by which groups communicate with candidates, principally by giving money or goods and services to the candidates' campaigns. In Chapter 4, we explore the ways that interest groups communicate with voters, their own members and supporters, and the larger electorate.

The introductory chapter places this activity in a broader context. The American political system has many unique features, and these provide the opportunity structures for groups to operate in elections. The groups' goals interact with these structures to produce broad strategies, and existing regulations and norms influence the specific tactics that groups choose to implement those strategies. The concluding chapter focuses on possible reforms of current laws that channel interest group activities in elections. We discuss a range of proposals that have been offered, lay out the values that underlie our own normative assessment of these proposals, and suggest areas where reform is needed.

A number of individuals assisted with the development and production of this book. We especially thank our colleagues Robert Biersack, John

Green, and Paul Herrnson, and we are grateful to the anonymous reviewers who critiqued our book proposal and completed manuscipt. CQ Press director Brenda Carter provided encouragement and support for this project from beginning through completion. We appreciate the very able help of production editors Nadine Steffan and Talia Greenberg. Sandy Chizinsky did a most thorough copyedit of the manuscript, Joyce Teague prepared the index, and Jessica Forman typeset the book.

Before writing this book we interviewed a number of individuals in the Washington, D.C., community who are active in interest group and party politics. Some are quoted in the pages that follow. All gave generously of their time and expertise and helped us immeasurably in the development of our own thinking on the role of interest groups in elections. We thank Walter Barbee (Family Foundation), Rich Bond (Bond and Associates), Jeff Butsky (National Federation of Independent Businesses), Bob Corrolla (Americans for Democratic Action), Jeff Eagan (Long Term Care Campaign), Dylan Glenn (Jensen and Co.), Patricia Goldman (WISH List), William Greener (1996 Republican National Convention), William Harris (1992 Republican National Convention), Heather Herndon (National Women's Political Caucus), Karen Hincks (National Committee to Preserve Social Security and Medicaid), Christine La Rocco (Bryce Harlow Foundation), Hon. Larry La Rocco (former member of Congress), Gregg Lebell (Interfaith Alliance), Mitchell Lester (EMILY's List), Tanya Metaksa (NRA Institute for Legislative Action), Kim Mills (Human Rights Campaign), Rudy Oswald (George Meany Institute), Trey Richardson (National Association of Realtors), Peter Roff (GOPAC), Amy Simon (Women's Campaign Fund), Ann E.W. Stone (Republicans for Choice), James Wagoner (NARAL), and Paul Wilson (Wilson and Associates).

CHAPTER 1

Interest Groups and American Politics

In the 1996 elections, interest groups were both more active and more visible than ever before. They participated in both the Republican and Democratic primaries—sometimes recruiting candidates, sometimes backing challengers to the party favorite—and also struggled to influence party platforms. In the general election, interest groups supported candidates for the presidency, for Congress, and even for state legislatures and school boards: they distributed voters' guides in shopping malls, union halls, and churches and called members to urge them to support specific candidates. In a number of congressional districts, coalitions of interest groups spent millions of dollars on radio and television advertisements, often outspending the candidates themselves. And interest groups made record contributions to both presidential candidates and to party committees.

Well aware of the potential for gains in votes and contributions, candidates courted interest groups, sometimes making public statements designed specifically to attract endorsements. Early in the campaign, Republican presidential candidate Bob Dole spent more than a week defending the tobacco industry against charges that tobacco was addictive, at one point saying, "We know it's not good for kids. But a lot of other things aren't good. Drinking's not good. Some would say milk's not good" ("Clinton Assails Dole" 1996). Bill Clinton, for his part, made special appeals to teachers' unions and to feminist and environmental groups. Congressional candidates cultivated ties with the National Rifle Association (NRA) and Handgun Control, Inc., with anti-abortion and pro-choice groups, and with businesses and labor unions.

What leads interest groups to take such an active role in American elections? In a word, influence. Interest groups seek to influence governmental policies, and their leaders believe that participation in the electoral process can help achieve this goal. First, by helping to elect candidates who share their views, interest groups can change the personnel of government, thereby increasing the likelihood that the policies they support will be implemented. Second, by aiding incumbents in their reelection bids, interest groups can more easily approach policy makers to argue their cases.

Interest group strategies and tactics depend on two sets of factors: on the one hand, the legal regulations and common practices that govern electoral activity, and on the other, the goals and resources of the group. The combination of legal regulations and common practices creates an *opportunity structure*—the framework within which interest groups can conduct their electoral activities. The interaction of the opportunity structure with goals and resources creates the *strategic context* of elections. Interest groups choose broad strategies on the basis of their goals and resources and then choose among the tactics that are available under the rules.

Why are more interest groups active in elections in more ways than ever before? To begin with, there are simply more interest groups than there were in the past, and they are pursuing more diverse policy goals. Early in the twentieth century, most interest groups were economic organizations, such as corporations and labor unions, with fairly narrow goals—to maximize profits or wages and benefits, for example. Although these groups sought to influence government policy, influence was not an end in itself but a means of achieving specific goals. In contrast, the principal goal of the newer interest groups—often referred to as *citizens' groups*—is to influence public policy, and the leaders of many of these groups view political action as the principal means of achieving policy goals. Although the goals of any one group may be narrow, collectively these new groups have taken on an extraordinary array of domestic and foreign policy issues, from banning abortions to limiting product liability and from selling weapons to Saudi Arabia to maintaining a trade embargo against Cuba.

The vast majority of citizens' groups currently active in Washington were created since the 1960s (Walker 1983). The wave of interest group formation that began in that decade—and continues, more moderately, in the 1990s—springs largely from major social movements—principally the civil rights, feminist, gay and lesbian rights, and Christian right movements, although there are also a number of interest groups that focus on single issues such as abortion or gun control. However, both single-issue groups and those that have sprung from social movements are highly active in electoral politics.

A second factor driving growth in interest group activity is the expansion of government involvement in everyday life. Legislation in the 1960s protecting citizens from discrimination on the basis of race or sex spurred the development of interest groups among minorities and women. The creation of Medicare in 1965 had a similar effect among older Americans. Growth among environmental groups occurred both before and after the passage of legislation to guarantee clean air and water, to protect endangered species, and to protect wetlands. Government regulations of the past four decades have also greatly affected how corporations do business. As a consequence, corporations are much more active in politics than they were before 1960.

Third, technology has made it much easier for interest groups to participate in electoral politics. Consider, for example, what would once have been a virtually impossible task: producing and mailing thousands of specially targeted materials two weeks before an election. Today, all any group needs is a Pentium computer, a good color printer, a minimum of expertise, and a long weekend. Technology has made it possible to identify the twenty closest congressional races, to match the zip codes of interest group members against congressional districts, and to produce targeted mailings just in time to sway members' votes.

A BRIEF HISTORY OF INTEREST GROUPS

Although interest groups are indeed more active in American elections than at any time in U.S. history, their participation in electoral politics is as old as the nation itself. In 1757, local merchants donated liquor to bribe voters in George Washington's run for election to the Virginia House of Burgesses (Sabato 1984). Religious groups were deeply involved in the party cleavages of the nineteenth century (Howe 1980; Swierenga 1980), in debates over removing Native Americans from their territory, and in controversies over slavery.

The election of 1896 was a watershed for interest group involvement in electoral politics. Mark Hanna, a Cleveland industrialist, contributed $100,000 (equivalent to more than $1 million today) to Republican William McKinley's presidential campaign; more important, however, Hanna *organized* the campaign. While McKinley sat greeting visitors on his front porch in Canton, Ohio, Hanna recruited and sent off on tour an army of some 1,400 pro-McKinley speakers. Hanna also raised record amounts for McKinley—between $35 million and $100 million in current dollars—by assessing banks and corporations a fee based on their assets. Standard Oil and J. P. Morgan gave $250,000 each (Baida 1992). While Democratic nominee William Jennings Bryan mobilized farmers, workers, and evangelical Christians, the Grand Old Party tapped the deep pockets of corporate America, outspending the Democrats by perhaps as much as twenty to one. By the early twentieth century, interest groups had become increasingly involved in elections, spurring efforts to regulate their activities. In 1907, the Tilman Act banned direct corporate and bank contributions to campaigns, but business found other ways of channeling money to candidates.

As interest groups increased in number and influence, they made their presence felt in both the Democratic and Republican Parties. Populist and progressive groups made their way into the Democratic Party, especially in states such as Wisconsin and Iowa. Newly formed labor unions allied themselves with the Democrats, and small and large businesses became core groups in the Republican base. Immigrants became part of the Democratic Party machine, while nativist groups—including the Ku Klux Klan—were active in Republican politics. Eventually, the New Deal coalition defined the Democratic Party as a collection of diverse groups—including labor, Catholics and Jews, racial minorities, and southerners—while the GOP established a strong constituency among both large and small businesses.

Although party organizations remained strong and party leaders continued to control nominations, interest groups were increasingly active and visible members of party coalitions. By midcentury, the two dominant political parties had established comfortable relations with interest groups: parties chose candidates and developed platforms, and interest groups backed the party nominees. But in the 1960s, the landscape abruptly changed.

There was an explosion in the formation of groups that represented not just economic interests, but other policy issues. In 1986, Kay Lehman Schlozman and John Tierney reported that a majority of civil rights' groups and more than three-fourths of citizens' groups, social welfare groups, and poor peoples' organizations had been founded since 1960 (Schlozman and Tierney 1986, 75). In the years since this study, the growth of policy-oriented groups has slowed somewhat, but the overall trend has continued.

Citizens committed to the broad social movements of the 1960s and early 1970s—in particular, the civil rights, antiwar, and feminist movements—surged into the Democratic Party, demanding representation and a voice in party policy. During the 1968 Democratic National Convention, the party establishment kept the newcomers out, and they marched by the thousands in the streets of Chicago. By 1972, the party had changed its regulations to allow interest groups greater influence on party nominations. At about the same time, changes in campaign finance laws led corporations and ideological groups to become involved in financing electoral campaigns. From the 1970s onward, interest groups were actively engaged in all stages and aspects of electoral contests.

The 1996 elections may well have marked the beginning of yet another era. Interest groups poured record amounts of money into campaigns. The funds often came directly from the treasuries of corporations—and, to a much smaller extent, from labor unions and citizens' groups. Perhaps more important, coalitions of interest groups mounted their own independent campaigns on behalf of candidates in specially targeted House races, spending millions of dollars on advertising that defined candidates' positions on issues and attacked their opponents' records and even their character.

These events may portend a change from elections centered on candidates to elections centered on interest group politics. The precise contours of this new system are not well defined, but it is possible that coalitions of interest groups will assume even more quasi-party functions in the future, including specialization in particular electoral activities. Already, the National Committee for an Effective Congress, which is affiliated with the coalition of liberal and Democratic groups, focuses on producing information to help candidates target their electoral activities (Herrnson 1994). In the coalition of conservatives and Republicans, the Christian Coalition specializes in distributing voters' guides in the churches. More important, many observers—political scientists, party officials, journalists, and policy makers—worry that interest groups may establish themselves as the primary source of communication with voters, drowning out the voices of political parties and even of the candidates themselves. Such a shift would damage the accountability of candidates in American elections and further weaken the parties.

To explore the role of interest groups in America fully, we first describe the diversity of interest groups and the nature of their political goals. Next, we examine varying views of the role of interest groups in American politics. We then consider the ways in which the unique characteristics of the American electoral system create opportunities for electoral involvement by interest groups. Finally, we explore the laws and regulations that regulate interest group activity in elections.

DIVERSE GROUPS, DIVERSE GOALS

Rhetoric about "special interests" has succeeded in persuading many Americans that interest groups play a devious and damaging role in American democracy. Candidates inevitably attack the "special interests" that support their opponents while welcoming contributions and endorsements from the "organized citizens" who are members of their own coalitions. In 1984, President Ronald Reagan enjoyed the support of much of corporate America and of citizens' groups that included the Veterans of Foreign Wars, the NRA, and the Moral Majority. Nonetheless, because Democratic challenger Walter Mondale had the support of unions, environmental groups, feminists, and civil rights organizations, Reagan successfully attacked Mondale as the "candidate of special interests." In the 1996 presidential campaign, Bob Dole attacked Bill Clinton for receiving support from trial lawyers, while Clinton attacked Dole for receiving support from the tobacco lobby. Independent candidate Ross Perot, meanwhile, claimed that the nominees of both major parties were influenced by special interests.

For many years, the National Election Studies have asked citizens whether they believe that "the government is pretty much run by a few big interests looking out for themselves or that it is run for the benefit of all the people." In 1996, 72 percent of respondents replied that the government is run by a few big interests. In a 1997 survey conducted by the Pew Research Center for the People and the Press, special interests were rated roughly even with "international terrorism" as the greatest threat to the nation's future (Pew 1997).

Ironically, many Americans who fear the power of interest groups are themselves members or supporters of such groups. Interest groups are simply collections of individuals who seek to influence public policy. Many small local organizations are interest groups. Consider, for example, two groups organized in Fairfax County, Virginia: Citizens United to Preserve

Huntley Meadow was organized to protect a small wetlands park—home to herons, bitterns, beaver, and raccoons and the site of beautiful sunsets—from a proposed road that the group believes will drain oil into the watershed. The Family Friendly Libraries group was formed to protest the inclusion of a gay newspaper among other community publications distributed free of charge at public libraries. Both organizations have attracted a number of committed activists, along with a somewhat larger group of less involved members, and have succeeded in drawing public attention to their causes.

Interest groups also include large organizations: environmental groups such as the Sierra Club and Friends of the Earth are interest groups, and so are anti-abortion and pro-choice groups such as Operation Rescue and the National Abortion and Reproductive Rights Action League (NARAL). The NRA and Handgun Control, Inc., are interest groups, as are the National Organization for Women (NOW), Concerned Women for America, the Children's Defense Fund, the National Council of Churches, and the National Association for the Advancement of Colored People (NAACP).

Interest groups focused primarily on economic policy include corporations both large and small, from AT&T to the thousands of small companies with only a handful of employees; umbrella business organizations, such as the U.S. Chamber of Commerce and the National Federation of Independent Businesses (NFIB); trade associations, such as the National Petroleum Institute, that represent entire sectors of the corporate economy; large national labor unions and small local unions; and professional organizations, such as the American Bar Association (ABA), the American Medical Association (AMA), and the American Political Science Association (APSA).

Whether an organization constitutes an interest group in our definition depends critically on whether it seeks to influence government policy. An Elvis fan club is not an interest group, but if the members approach government officials to support an Elvis stamp, it becomes an interest group. Similarly, churches become interest groups when they lobby government or seek to influence elections. Many churches confine their activities to the religious arena, but some endorse candidates, others mount voter registration drives, and still others collect petitions against abortion or in favor of national health insurance. Entire religious denominations constitute interest groups when they lobby government—as many often do (Hertzke 1988).

Probably the best canvas of active interest groups was conducted by Schlozman and Tierney (1986). Figure 1-1, which shows the distribution of interest groups by type, indicates clearly that business interests dominate

FIGURE 1-1
Interest Groups by Type

Percentage

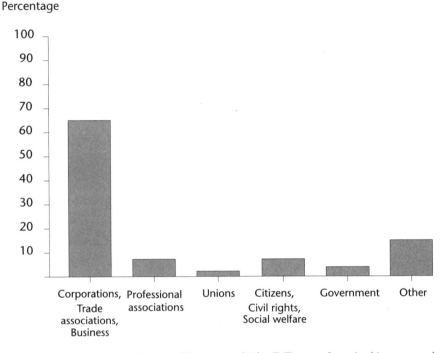

Source: Adapted from Kay Lehman Schlozman and John T. Tierney, *Organized Interests and American Democracy* (New York: Harper and Row, 1986), 67.

the universe of interest groups represented in Washington: professional associations, unions, and citizens' groups together constitute less than a quarter of the total number of business groups. Although there has been no thorough census of interest groups in the years since this study, the share of citizens' groups has probably increased modestly, but the general proportions shown in the figure are likely to have remained unchanged.

Within the broad category of interest groups are four distinct types of groups—business groups, professional associations, labor unions, and citizens' groups—each with its own agenda and goals. Business groups include corporations, trade associations, and business associations. Corporations often approach government for assistance with particular problems—to obtain relief from regulatory controls, to obtain protection from product liability suits or from foreign or domestic competition, or to seek government contracts. Although the resources of large corporations enable them to get involved in elections, many corporations are too small to play roles of any significance in electoral politics. Trade associations, which represent entire industries, seek policies that will benefit a particular type of business—construction, oil, or tobacco, for example. Business associations, such as the U.S. Chamber of Commerce and the NFIB, seek to influence economic policy: to lower taxes, reduce regulation, protect American patents and copyrights, and keep labor costs low.

Professional associations vary widely in their goals. Most seek some protection from competition through licensing and control over professional credentials. Teachers' associations, for example, want to ensure that only those with education degrees can teach in public schools; lawyers' groups want to ensure that certain services can be provided only by lawyers. Professional associations also promote policies that will economically benefit their members, such as when the AMA promotes certain policies regarding government health insurance programs. Professional associations also support broader policy changes, however. For example, the ABA proposes model legal codes for the states and rates presidential nominees for federal court, and the AMA lobbies for antismoking legislation.

Labor unions generally support policies that promote job creation, protect union workers from economic loss during recessions, protect union workers from job loss when factories move overseas, regulate employer-worker relations, and require employers to provide health insurance benefits. Unions also favor policies that benefit retired workers, such as funding for Medicare and Social Security. At times, unions have joined larger coalitions to promote civil rights.

Citizens' groups represent an almost bewildering array of causes: legal protection for African American, Hispanic, gay, lesbian, and disabled citizens; policies that make it easier (or harder) for women to work outside the home; policies for and against gun control; policies that provide greater environmental protection or less government regulation; funding for abortion or for child welfare; the abolition or the use of capital punishment.

Some citizens' groups are part of broad, decentralized social movements that hope to shape society according to their particular visions. In their early stages, social movements are usually intensely ideological, spawning a number of competing organizations, each of which seeks to define an ideology and an agenda for the movement. Although activist leaders may be reluctant to compromise during this stage, the intensity associated with the early development of a social movement eventually subsides, usually leaving behind a large, fairly moderate organization and several smaller, more radical groups. The civil rights and feminist movements are examples of relatively successful movements that have become more moderate with time and that now work within the system as mainstream interest groups. Activists from the Christian right, a social movement in its more ideological phase, are often unwilling to compromise with GOP moderates over policy or politics.

It is important to understand the distinction between an interest group and a political party. One textbook defines political parties as "organizations that seek to control government by recruiting, nominating, and electing their members to public office" and interest groups as "organizations that try to achieve at least some of their goals with government assistance" (Welch et al. 1998). These definitions are useful in distinguishing between the Republican National Committee and the U.S. Chamber of Commerce, but many organizations fall into a "gray zone" between political parties and interest groups.

Consider, for example, the Christian Coalition, which seeks, among other things, to recruit conservative Christians and help them run for office. Although it might seem to fit the definition of a political party, it is more accurately viewed as an interest group that is closely but informally associated with one faction within the Republican Party. Similarly, Americans for Tax Reform, founded by a longtime Republican activist, mobilizes voters to support Republican candidates; and GOPAC, founded by House Speaker Newt Gingrich, R-Ga., seeks to elect more Republicans to office and recruits and trains candidates to run. In this volume, organizations such as the Christian Coalition and Americans for Tax Reform will be defined as interest groups because they seek to promote specific policies by electing and influencing members of one political party. Organizations such as GOPAC and the Democratic Leadership Council, in contrast, will be defined as quasi-party organizations—first, because they are composed almost entirely of party activists, and second, because their primary goal is to promote the party, not specific policies.

THE ONE, THE FEW, OR THE MANY: INTEREST GROUPS AND AMERICAN POLITICS

The framers of the Constitution anticipated and welcomed a vigorous role for interest groups in electoral politics and governing. When James Madison, our chief constitutional architect, warned of the "mischief of factions," he meant that the greatest threat of factions—or what we commonly call interest groups—was the potential for one or a few of them to become too large and powerful—to the point of being able to control the levers of government and destroy the rights and liberties of others. Madison's cure was the creation of a large federal republic in which numerous diverse interests would flourish and in which no one group could become so overwhelmingly powerful as to threaten the rights and liberties of numerically smaller or less powerful groups. In a competitive policy environment, numerous groups would counter each other, and public policy, in the ideal, would represent compromises among competing interests and reflect "the public good."

Scholars have debated for generations whether the Madisonian solution has succeeded in preventing one or a few groups from dominating American politics. Some social scientists see corporate interests as forming a single dominant coalition that routinely triumphs in political struggles; others see an evolving two-party system of interest groups allied with the two major political parties; pluralists suggest that a multitude of groups, representing many Americans, compete with one another to define the public agenda, and no one group or coalition dominates politics.

Is the universe of American interest groups dominated by a single coalition of business interests, or is it characterized by thousands of competing groups? Social scientists have long argued the point. As noted earlier, business groups are indeed numerically dominant and have important financial advantages. However, it is also true that many Americans are members of interest groups. One comprehensive study (Verba, Schlozman, and Brady 1995) showed that 79 percent of Americans are members of some kind of voluntary association, including hobby and sports groups. Sixty-one percent are associated with a group that they described as taking a stand on politics. Such broad citizen involvement would seem to support a pluralist view of interest groups.

Although the authors report that interest group membership and activism are more prevalent among those with greater resources (such as income and education), they also found that involvement in interest groups and other voluntary associations builds civic skills that lead to more effective citizenship. Some institutions—most notably churches—build these skills among those who may initially be at a substantial disadvantage in relation to the political process, and some issues—particularly abortion—mobilize citizens who would otherwise be unlikely to join or form groups.

Empirical research thus supports some of the claims of the critics of interest groups and some of the claims of their supporters. The interest group universe is dominated by business interests, which along with professional associations and labor unions generally seek economic benefits for their members. But some interest groups do represent disadvantaged segments of the population, and by encouraging their members to become involved in politics, educated about issues and candidates, volunteer in campaigns, and develop the kinds of skills that make them more effective citizens, these groups may strengthen democratic representation.

We have seen that there are many types of interest groups active in American elections, representing myriad causes. The nature of interest group involvement in electoral activity is constrained by the political system and by the laws, regulations, and practices that create opportunity structures. We next turn to a discussion of the political system and the opportunities it creates for interest group involvement in elections.

INTEREST GROUPS AND THE AMERICAN POLITICAL SYSTEM

Interest groups' high level of involvement in American elections stems, in part, from distinctive characteristics of American government, political parties, and elections. First, governmental decision making offers multiple incentives and opportunities for influencing policy. Second, the major U.S. parties are permeable to outside interests, enabling interest group activists to obtain powerful positions within local, state, and national party organizations. Third, American elections are unique: they are much more frequent than those of most other Western democracies, and far smaller percentages of citizens vote. Moreover, American elections are candidate centered: candidates must decide to run, raise their own funds, assemble their own coalitions, and reach voters with carefully targeted messages—all of which occurs outside the formal party structure. The three sections that follow consider each of these characteristics in more detail.

Characteristics of American Government

At the same time that our federal system creates incentives for interest group involvement, it also places demands on interest groups, which must work within the system in order to successfully influence policy. First, because policy can be made at the national, state, and local levels, interest groups are generally called upon to be active at all three levels. Consider, for example, gun control policy. The NRA and Handgun Control, Inc., are committed to influencing gun control legislation in Congress, in state legislatures, and in county commissions and local councils. To do so, these organizations must have friends at each level of government, and being active in elections at all levels is one way to ensure this. Sometimes a victory at one level of government can be overturned at another level: for example, Handgun Control, Inc., has won a number of victories at the city level, and the NRA has therefore been lobbying for state laws to prohibit local governments from passing stringent gun control laws (Bruce and Wilcox 1998).

Second, interest groups are well aware that local councils and state legislatures constitute a "pipeline" of potential candidates for the House of Representatives. Thus, they often participate in state and local races with the intention of cultivating and training potential candidates for national office.

Third, the division of powers between the executive and legislative branches means that interest groups must try to cultivate access to both the president and Congress. Given that the executive and legislative branches have different constituencies, timetables, and interests, this is a difficult enough task, but it has been made even more complex during the past forty years because the two branches have often been under the control of different parties. Today, interest groups with access to the Republicans in the House and Senate need the signature of a Democratic president before their bills can become law. The House is a predominantly urban and suburban body where the majority party can generally pass what it pleases, but the Senate has a disproportionately rural slant and has rules that allow any senator—including members of the minority party—to delay voting on a measure indefinitely.

Fourth, because members of Congress are not bound to vote for the policies of party leaders but are independent actors, even those of the minority party are in a position to help or hurt an interest group's policy agenda. Any member of the House or Senate can introduce a bill drafted in consultation with an interest group and offer amendments in committee or on the floor to make the bill more palatable to interest groups. When a bill is up for a vote, members of Congress may vote however they choose. In the Senate, any member can put a "hold" on a bill, delaying a vote perhaps indefinitely.

Thus, interest groups often bolster their lobbying efforts by engaging in electoral activities. By helping members of Congress in elections, interest groups hope to establish relationships with senators and representatives—and to get some return on their investment in the form of public policy actions. On occasion, relationships cultivated through electoral activity enable interest groups to build coalitions in support of their policy positions, even over the objections of party leaders.

Finally, the U.S. government is perhaps more willing than that of many other countries to distribute particularistic economic benefits to interest groups. Appropriations, tax, and even substantive bills such as highway bills are generally filled with specific language benefiting one or more companies or interest groups. Corporations get government contracts, special tax provisions, and exemptions from regulations (or, more commonly, delays in implementing regulations), all of which can affect their profits. In addition, members of Congress and occasionally even presidents intercede with the bureaucracy in an attempt to win favorable treatment for particular groups. The opportunity to obtain specific economic benefits is yet another incentive for interest groups to develop close relationships with policy makers—and one important way to do so is through electoral politics.

Characteristics of American Parties

Like the American government, American political parties differ from their counterparts in other democracies. In many countries, parties are closely linked with one or a few interests that they can be said to represent. In Europe, labor unions are represented by labor or social democratic parties, the Catholic Church speaks through Christian democratic parties, environmentalists have formed "green" parties, and very conservative citizens are represented by "new radical right" parties. In Israel, orthodox religious groups have their own political parties. In some countries, interest groups are represented by distinct sectors of a party. In Mexico, for example, the Partido Revolucionario Institucionalizado (PRI) has separate sectors representing agriculture, workers, and students.

In the United States, however, the parties have established relationships with a variety of interest groups that make up their core constituencies, but they also interact with groups that are nonpartisan or that are willing to back candidates of either party. Democratic Party activists include members of labor unions, civil rights organizations, feminist organizations, environmental groups, and consumer protection organizations. Republican

Party activists include small-business owners, conservative Christians, and advocates of gun rights. Big business provides significant support to both parties, and although the executives of most large companies prefer Republican lawmakers, they are usually willing to do business with whoever controls the governmental agenda. The loose coalitions of interest groups that make up American parties often pull parties in different directions: within the Democratic Party, unions and environmental groups may clash over clean air standards for industry; within the Republican Party, conservative Christians and the business community may differ over policies enabling women to participate more fully in the paid workforce or over the teaching of evolution in high school biology classes.

Because interest groups have resources—mailing lists, newsletters, conventions, and volunteers—that can help political parties reach out to group members and other voters, parties often rely on interest groups to help them communicate with voters, often working closely with particular groups to develop and distribute distinctive messages targeting group members. When GOP leaders want to get the word out to white evangelical voters that theirs is the party of moral conservatism, they ask the Christian Coalition to carry the message in its publications, to distribute voters' guides in conservative churches, and to allow party leaders to speak at the organization's annual convention. Similarly, Democratic officials rely on unions to reach workers, on feminist organizations to reach working women, and on environmental groups to reach voters who are concerned about pollution.

Perhaps the most distinctive feature of American parties and elections is that party leaders play only a small role in selecting candidates. Through party primaries, caucuses, and conventions, interest groups can help to determine which candidates win nomination and can even work to nominate activists and members from their own groups. Although party officials are usually neutral in intraparty contests, interest groups—both individually and in coalition with others—are extremely active in aiding one candidate over another.

On rare occasions, party leaders may personally endorse candidates in primaries or even conventions, only to see their favorite defeated by a candidate who has the backing of powerful interest groups. For example, in a 1996 party primary for the seat he had vacated to run for the presidency, Bob Dole backed incumbent U.S. senator Sheila Frahm, a pro-choice but fiscally conservative former state senate majority leader who had been appointed by the governor to complete Dole's term. Largely because of efforts by Christian right activists, the election went to social conservative Sam Brownback, a one-term representative. In 1998, House Speaker Newt Gingrich and former president Gerald Ford recruited a moderate, pro-choice GOP member of the California assembly to run in the primary for a U.S. House seat vacated by the death of an incumbent. Christian right activists recruited a conservative, anti-abortion candidate, spent more than $100,000 in advertising, and saw their candidate win the primary.

Finally, unlike many European parties, which receive most or all of their campaign money from the government, American parties must raise their own money from individual and group contributions. Interest groups provide much of the money for parties through a variety of legal mechanisms. Money from interest groups helps fund party electoral activities, as well as buildings, computers, and party workers' salaries. Interest groups also contribute to party foundations and think tanks that develop policy proposals for party leaders.

Characteristics of American Elections

Elections are a necessary component of democracy, but democracies implement elections in very different ways. In most countries, elections are held at regular intervals and generally occur at the same time, both for national executive and legislative offices and for regional and local government posts. Moreover, campaigns in most countries are relatively short: in Britain, for example, the 1996 campaign lasted six weeks and included all the seats in the national legislature and most local races.

In the United States, in contrast, elections are held almost continuously. Consider, for example, the electoral calendar in Virginia, where in 1997 there were party conventions, primaries, and general elections for the state legislature and three statewide offices (governor, lieutenant governor, attorney general); in 1998 there will be conventions, primaries, and general elections for members of the House; in 1999 there will be conventions, primaries, and general elections for the state legislature; and in 2000 there will be conventions, primaries, and general elections for the presidency and both houses of Congress. This adds up to eight regularly scheduled elections in four years, and many party nominating conventions. In addition, local governments will hold hundreds of contests to elect members of county boards, local councils, and school boards as well as other important officials.

Because members of the House of Representatives stand for election every two years, representatives are constantly running for reelection—raising money, addressing voters, refining their images and their messages. And their challengers sometimes begin campaigning more than a year before the election. Senators, who are elected for six-year terms, generally campaign for at least two years, and some focus on fund raising throughout their terms. Even before a new president is sworn into office, prospective candidates from the other major party may drop in on the early presidential caucus and primary states of Iowa and New Hampshire to "test the political waters."

Another distinctive characteristic of American elections is that they are candidate centered. In most democracies, parties run against each other with the help of their candidates; in the United States, candidates run against each other with the support of their parties. Indeed, some candidates do not even use party labels during their campaigns and attempt to distance themselves from other candidates of their party. In 1994, Rudolph Giuliani, the Republican mayor of New York, endorsed Democratic candidate Mario Cuomo for the governorship. Elizabeth McCoughey, the lieutenant governor of New York who was elected that year as a Republican, announced in midterm that she was a Democrat and would seek future office from her new party. In a parliamentary system, where voters elect parties, not individuals, McCoughey would have had to resign her position. In our system, she was able to keep not only her position but also some of her Republican benefactors—including U.S. senator Alfonse D'Amato—who pledged to continue supporting her. Meanwhile, some of McCoughey's former Democratic opponents refused to welcome her.

Although American elections provide opportunities for individual candidates to adopt distinctive campaign themes, they also place significant burdens on candidates. In most other democracies, party leaders choose the candidates. The party finances the elections, chooses the issues to frame the campaign, and appeals to voters through party organizations and mass media. The party platform includes pledges for all party members; and, once elected, a legislator is expected to vote the party line on all or most issues.

In the United States, candidates must declare their intention to run and seek their party's nomination in a primary election, caucus, or convention. Their campaigns are financed with little help from the party, often with significant amounts of their own money in their first run for office. They must assemble their own electoral coalition—including and going beyond party loyalists in their state or district—and they must reach well-defined groups of voters with precisely targeted messages. They must take positions on a variety of issues—positions that may differ greatly from those of other party candidates or even from the official party platform.

The difficulties of running a candidate-centered campaign render interest groups obvious allies. Interest groups can recruit candidates and encourage them to run, help finance their campaigns, and assist them in selecting campaign themes. By providing access to special communication channels such as newsletters and group gatherings, interest groups can also help candidates reach interest group members effectively and inexpensively. When interest groups work closely with candidates during campaigns, they have opportunities to "encourage" them to adopt certain positions on issues of concern to the group—from abortion to the flat tax to aid to the United Nations. Interest groups that succeed in recruiting and assisting sufficient numbers of candidates from outside the party mainstream may be able to redefine the philosophy, goals, or agenda of the party as a whole.

A third unique characteristic of American elections is the low rate of voter turnout. In most Western democracies, substantial majorities of eligible voters cast ballots in national elections; turnout in national elections is over 80 percent in most European countries, and only in Switzerland do fewer than two-thirds of eligible voters cast ballots. In the United States, in contrast, fewer than half of those eligible voted in 1996, and in the 1994 congressional elections the figure was only 39 percent.

Low levels of voter turnout create opportunities for organized groups to greatly influence election outcomes. In the 1994 elections, for example, most candidates were elected by the votes of fewer than one-third of all eligible voters, and in many states fewer than one-fifth of eligible voters supported the average winning candidate (Center for Voting and Democracy: http://www.ultranet.com/~el/vdr95/repindex.html). With such slim margins, interest groups that can successfully mobilize their members to support a particular candidate may well be able to swing an election outcome. Voter mobilization efforts by unions, African American churches, and the Christian right are vital to the success of many candidates. Indeed, parties sometimes provide money to interest groups to help them mobilize voters, as the Republicans did in 1996 when they gave over $4 million to the conservative group Americans for Tax Reform.

Finally, American elections are nearly always winner-take-all contests in single-member districts. To see why this creates an incentive for interest groups to participate in elections, consider the consequences of a 2 percent shift under two different systems: if German labor unions succeeded in increasing by 2 percent the vote share of the German Social Democratic

Party, that party would gain approximately 2 percent of the seats in the Bundestag, the German parliament, because a party's share of seats in the legislature is proportional to its percentage of the popular vote. In the United States, where representation is not proportional but is based on single-member districts, a 2 percent increase in the Democratic Party's share of the vote for the U.S. House would likely enable Democrats to regain control of that body, because the increase would allow a number of Democratic candidates in close races to win the seats. Thus, a modest aggregate swing in votes may allow one party to capture most of the close contests in the United States, resulting in a much larger swing in seats. In 1994, the Republicans won control of the House by a net swing of less than 2 percent of the popular vote.

REGULATIONS, GOALS, AND RESOURCES

Taken together, the distinctive features of American government, parties, and elections give interest groups many opportunities and incentives to participate in election campaigns. Yet the precise form of their electoral involvement is channeled by government regulations that affect the ways in which interest groups use their resources to achieve their goals. These regulations will be discussed in detail in the chapters that follow, but we will look briefly in this section at the laws and regulations that influence how interest groups interact with parties, with candidates, and with voters.

The U.S. Constitution does not mention political parties, and relatively few federal regulations affect parties. Although state governments do regulate parties, the Supreme Court has limited states' ability to interfere with parties' internal affairs. However, the rules of the national, state, and local parties, which are sometimes influenced by state and local law, do have a profound impact on the opportunity structures that interest groups encounter.

Most important is the structure of the nomination process. Parties can choose among various types of primary elections, caucuses, and conventions to nominate their candidates, and rules pertaining to the nomination process influence the ability of interest groups to sway the outcome. Party primaries, for example, generally attract a sizable minority of eligible voters, making it more difficult for interest groups to dominate the process. Because conventions and caucuses often involve only a small minority of party supporters, they provide interest groups with much greater opportunities for influence. Thus, interest groups are often more active in recruit-ment and nomination politics in states with caucuses and conventions than in states with primary elections.

In Minnesota, in 1994, for example, conservative Christians mobilized their followers to help nominate former Republican legislator Allan Quist instead of incumbent Republican governor Arne Carlson. It is unusual for a major constituency group in a political party to work to deny the nom-ination to a popular incumbent, but Quist's long opposition to abortion had won the support of anti-abortion groups. Party moderates considered Quist an extremist, and many of his statements and policy positions had lent credibility to the charge. At the party convention, Quist defeated Carl-son by two to one, winning the party's endorsement; but in the primary election, which actually selected the nominee, Carlson prevailed by the same margin.

National party rules also affect interest groups' strategies. Both parties have rules governing participation on committees and make it relatively easy for interest groups to influence the platform process. The power of grassroots organizations to influence the GOP platform was evident in 1996, when anti-abortion groups worked to ensure places for their activists on the platform committee and succeeded in deflecting efforts by party moderates to adopt a plank pledging tolerance of differing viewpoints on abortion. Public and private polls both show that there are more pro-choice than anti-abortion GOP voters, but anti-abortion groups dominate convention politics and platform committees.

Other rules that affect interest groups' strategies are portions of the tax code that determine which groups can receive tax-deductible contribu-tions from members. Organizations that do not lobby Congress but that advocate positions to executive agencies and provide information to Con-gress can qualify for 501(c)(3) status, which exempts them from income tax and allows contributors to deduct donations from their taxes. Such orga-nizations cannot take part in partisan electoral activity, although they may provide citizens with nonpartisan information about issues.

Organizations find 501(c)(3) status highly advantageous because it allows them not only to receive large contributions from wealthy donors in search of tax breaks, but also to receive money from tax-exempt foun-dations, which are legally prohibited from giving to lobbying groups. The Christian Coalition is thus permitted to issue "nonpartisan" voters' guides that do not endorse candidates but that do include unflattering pho-tographs of Democrats and that often distort their positions to ensure that conservative Christian voters pick the "right" (that is, Republican) candidate. When the Sierra Club was stripped of its 501(c)(3) status in the 1960s because of lobbying activities, it established the Sierra Club Foundation, a separate organization that does not lobby or engage in campaign activity and therefore qualifies for 501(c)(3) status. The Sierra Club continues to lobby from within the main organization and runs an affiliated PAC that raises money from club members and contributes to candidates' campaigns.

Finally, electoral activity is regulated by the Federal Election Campaign Act, as amended in 1974 and again in 1979, and by Supreme Court interpretations of the free speech provisions of the First Amendment. Campaign finance regulations are quite complex and will be discussed more fully in Chapters 3 and 4. Briefly, to facilitate "party building" and to help candidates for state and local office, interest group treasuries can donate unlimited amounts of "soft money" to parties. As long as interest groups do not call explicitly for the election of a particular candidate, they can also spend unlimited amounts to advocate positions to the general electorate.

Interest groups can also form PACs, which can raise funds from members to be spent in any of a number of ways: the money can be given to candidates directly, or it can be spent by the PAC itself, in the form of independent expenditures, to advocate the election or defeat of particular candidates. PAC activities must be disclosed to the Federal Election Commission, and the funds involved must fit within certain contribution limits.

Some interest groups create byzantine organizational structures to deal with the various provisions of campaign finance laws. For example, organizations engaged in "independent expenditures" cannot coordinate their actions with the candidates on whose behalf they are spending. To avoid being accused of coordinating expenditures, interest groups that provide advice to candidates as an in-kind contribution may go so far as to establish a separate organizational unit (sometimes even setting it up in a different city) to provide this advice.

Characteristics of the American political system and applicable regulations combine to establish an opportunity structure for interest group involvement in elections. Faced with a set of opportunities and constraints, interest groups decide—largely on the basis of their goals and resources—whether and how to become involved in electoral politics.

Interest groups vary widely in the types of policies they seek to influence and in the frequency with which they attempt to do so. Many groups seek policies that provide a direct economic benefit such as higher wages, higher corporate profits, or the power to issue professional licenses. When firms or professional or trade associations seek special treatment from government—a contract, a tax break, regulatory relief—they need access to incumbents. Although Republicans are generally more willing than Democrats to support corporations, incumbents of both parties routinely try to help firms and professional and trade associations in their states and districts. Since a tax break from a Democrat is worth as much as a tax break from a Republican, many interest groups seek access to incumbents of either party, as long as officeholders have the power to insert into legislation special language that will help the group meet its goals. Such goals generally lead to strategies that focus on financial contributions from PACs and from corporate executives and their families.

Labor unions and business associations tend to be interested in broader policies affecting the entire economy. Because there are clear distinctions between the parties on a number of economic issues—levels of taxation and regulation, for example—interest groups tend to form close ties with one party or the other. Organized labor is more than a constituency group within the Democratic Party; it also performs many traditional party functions—organizing fund raising, conducting issues research, and sending campaign professionals into the field. The NFIB is rapidly assuming a similar role for the GOP. The precise boundaries between such organizations and party committees are unclear, and campaign professionals often work first for one group and then for the other.

Other organizations seek noneconomic benefits from a variety of policies, from those that affect the quality of the environment to reproductive choice to the types of books and magazines sold in bookstores. Some of these organizations seek access to both parties, helping candidates who support their position regardless of party. Indeed, primarily so that it can maintain its bipartisan stance, the Sierra Club even practices "affirmative action" for Republicans, endorsing GOP incumbents with acceptable environmental records even when they are opposed by Democratic challengers with "greener" policy views (Cantor forthcoming). NARAL and the NRA back candidates from both parties, although the widening differences between the parties' positions on abortion and gun control mean that these groups generally support candidates of one party or the other (Patterson and Eakins 1998; Thomas forthcoming).

Still other ideological groups are closely linked with a single party. Although the Christian Coalition is technically bipartisan, in practice it supports only Republicans. GOP committees have helped fund voter mobilization efforts conducted by the National Right to Life Committee.

In some cases, the same ideological position may be represented by different groups associated with different parties. EMILY's List and WISH List (Women in the Senate and House) are two pro-choice PACs dedicated to electing more women to Congress, but the first supports only pro-choice Democratic women, while the second backs GOP women candidates.

Interest groups' strategies are also influenced by their resources: groups with substantial financial assets may make sizable contributions to parties and spend significant amounts to help elect candidates. The tobacco industry, for example, includes two firms that rank among the highest donors of soft money to both parties. Groups with large memberships—such as the American Federation of Labor–Congress of Industrial Organizations (AFL-CIO) and the NRA—work hard to communicate endorsements to their members and get them to the polls.

Interest groups that are well respected may strive to communicate their views to the wider electorate: one Sierra Club official refers to that organization's endorsement as the environmental version of the "Good Housekeeping Seal of Approval" (Cantor 1998). Interest groups that are part of large, enthusiastic social movements may channel activists into volunteer efforts for campaigns and recruit members to run for office. The Christian Coalition, for example, fields thousands of activists who work in campaigns, distribute voters' guides in churches, and sometimes run in Republican primaries. Finally, groups with considerable electoral skills often send professionals into campaigns and may mount independent campaigns on behalf of candidates. In the 1996 elections, labor unions and environmental groups had field staff assisting candidates in specially targeted races; these groups also undertook independent campaigns to advocate the defeat of many newly elected House Republicans.

STRATEGIES AND TACTICS

Interest groups are involved in all aspects of American elections, and many begin their work on the next campaign the day after election results are announced. Of the tactics they use in their electoral activities, many center on offering candidates access to their group's resources: money, advice, volunteer labor, and votes. In addition, interest groups work to influence the two major parties—partly by maintaining ongoing relationships with the parties, but sometimes more aggressively, by attempting to dominate party committees or to rewrite party rules and platforms to favor their interests. Interest groups also recruit and train candidates who seek nomination in the major parties. In general elections, they invest funds in communicating their endorsements to members and in targeting particular candidates for defeat.

Consider the range of activities undertaken by interest groups in the 1996 elections. Women's groups, including the National Women's Political Caucus, recruited women to run for local, state, and national office, often in coalition with other feminist organizations (see National Women's Political Caucus 1997b). Similarly, the Christian Coalition encouraged conservative Christians to run for school boards, state legislatures, and Congress; it was also involved in discussions with potential presidential candidates as they considered the decision to run.

Organizations such as the Free Congress Foundation provided training for candidates and campaign managers, offering advice on topics that ranged from how to raise money and assemble electoral coalitions to how to shake hands all day without experiencing too much pain. Anti-abortion groups distributed pamphlets to sympathetic candidates on how to finesse the abortion issue in public discussions. Advice to candidates was sometimes continuous; the Sierra Club placed its staff and volunteers directly into some campaigns, affording candidates ongoing access to their expertise.

Interest groups provided candidates with resources throughout the nomination process. Organizations such as EMILY's List contributed money to pro-choice women running in Democratic primaries; more important, they encouraged their members to contribute as well. Such gifts are almost always welcomed, although they can occasionally create problems: as Bob Dole sought the GOP nomination, he first accepted—then returned, then apologized for returning—a contribution from the Log Cabin Republicans, a gay and lesbian organization that was unpalatable to Dole's conservative Christian backers.

Interest groups gave more than cash: some provided services such as polls or information on targeting campaign communications to voters, and others encouraged their members to volunteer for campaigns. Interest groups also provided candidates with forums to address their members: nearly all prospective GOP presidential candidates addressed the annual Christian Coalition gathering in Washington, D.C., in 1995, and most candidates campaigned by traveling from one group-sponsored event to another. Overall, these efforts helped interest groups influence candidates fielded by both parties in the 1996 general elections.

Interest groups also worked closely with the parties, often in the context of long-established relationships. The National Committee on an Effective Congress provided the Democratic Party with information to help the party better target its communication and voter mobilization efforts (Herrnson 1994), while major corporate interests gave the Republicans (and, to a lesser extent, the Democrats) both hard and soft money contributions to help them reach voters. Labor unions exchanged tips on strategy with Democratic Party committees and launched voter contact drives to encourage their members to support Democratic candidates, while the Christian Coalition distributed voters' guides containing flattering photos and descriptions of Republican candidates and unflattering photos and descriptions of Democrats.

Perhaps more important, interest groups worked within both political parties to influence party rules and nominations. Interest group members ran for party office at the precinct, county, state, and national levels. By 1996, conservative Christian activists either dominated or had a significant role in thirty-one state Republican committees and in many county and precinct committees; and they provided the critical votes in the selection of the new national Republican Party chairman (Rozell and Wilcox 1995, 1997). Conservative Christian and anti-abortion groups also dominated the GOP platform committee, successfully repudiating an effort by party moderates and presidential nominee Bob Dole to include language calling for the party to tolerate differences of opinion on abortion. The Democratic convention was attended by large numbers of feminist and civil rights activists, union members, and trial lawyers—groups that traditionally work to influence the Democratic Party platform.

Many interest groups endorsed candidates in both primary and general elections. Labor union endorsements sent to all union members served as the basis for later voter mobilization efforts. Sierra Club endorsements of both Democrats and Republicans were communicated to members and the media, while the League of Conservation Voters (LCV) publicized the names of the "Dirty Dozen"—the twelve candidates with the worst environmental records. Groups such as the Christian Coalition, which could not officially endorse candidates because it claims tax-exempt status, nevertheless managed to signal their enthusiasm for particular candidates without making official endorsements.

During the general election, interest groups continued to provide candidates with access to the same kinds of resources they had made available during primary elections and caucuses: advice, services, volunteers, cash, and forums in which to address interest group members. Interest groups also communicated with the broader electorate to influence their votes. Labor unions and environmental groups spent millions to inform voters in selected congressional districts that incumbent Republicans had voted against social programs and the environment, while the NFIB led a coalition of organizations that spent millions to defend GOP incumbents. Interest groups also provided much of the muscle behind voter mobilization efforts: labor unions called their members to urge them to vote; and on the Sunday before the election, the Christian Coalition distributed millions of voters' guides in conservative churches.

Despite the apparent diversity of tactics, interest groups generally pursue a mix of two basic strategies: an *electoral strategy,* which is designed to change the personnel of government, and an *access,* or *legislative strategy,* which uses electoral activity as an adjunct to lobbying efforts. The electoral strategy is an attempt to increase the number of policy makers who share the group's policy views. When the leaders of the Business-Industry Political Action Committee (BIPAC) endorse a challenger in a House race, they are telling the business community that they are confident that the candidate, if elected, will vote for pro-business policies. When the leaders of the LCV refers to certain members of Congress as the Dirty Dozen, they are hoping to replace those members with others more sympathetic to environmental causes.

Groups most likely to use an electoral strategy are labor unions, citizens' groups, and social movement organizations. Such groups often attempt to influence party nominations by recruiting and supporting candidates in primary elections, sending delegates to party conventions to influence the platform, spending large sums in a few closely contested races where candidates take opposing stands on issues of special importance to the group, and mobilizing voters to help sway close contests. They make use of their special resources—their members, their activist core, their reputations, and any media support they can muster.

Often, however, interest groups assist candidates who are not involved in close races: PACs give money to committee chairs who face no serious competition; interest groups endorse candidates who are running unopposed or mount voter mobilization efforts for candidates whose victory is assured. Why bother? As noted earlier, interest groups seek not only to change the personnel of government but also to secure access to those who have the power to make or influence decisions—a cabinet member, a party leader, a committee chair. There are many ways to gain access to policy makers, but one important way is to develop an ongoing relationship through campaign aid. When interest groups pursue a legislative or access strategy—helping candidates and parties in order to secure time to make their argument before policy makers—whether the policy maker needs electoral help is of little concern. When Sen. Lloyd Bentsen, D-Texas, chaired the Senate Finance Committee in the 1980s, he hosted a $10,000-a-plate PAC breakfast providing interest group representatives with an opportunity to contribute to his reelection campaign and meet with him to discuss issues of concern. Bentsen was unlikely to face serious opposition in his next campaign, but the groups that chose to contribute were assured of his ear, at least during the breakfast, and those that chose not to contribute were less likely to be able to meet privately with the senator to discuss tax matters.[1] In fact, interest groups that pursue access strategies often prefer to contribute to candidates who are sure winners.

Corporations, trade associations, and professional associations are the most likely to emphasize an access strategy. Groups seeking access rarely participate in primary elections and do not usually undertake voter mobilization efforts. Their preferred tactics are, instead, to give substantial sums to party committees (often to both parties), to help finance party conventions, and to form PACs to give money to incumbents.

HOW THIS BOOK IS ORGANIZED

Interest group involvement in American elections takes myriad forms, and there are a number of ways to structure an examination of that involvement. This book focuses on communication: with whom are interest groups communicating, and to what end? Some of the activities of interest groups are aimed primarily at communicating with political parties, in order to influence the policies that the parties pursue. Recruiting and training candidates, working to elect candidates in primary elections and caucuses, working at party conventions, and placing group members in party office are all ways of influencing political parties, as are direct contributions to party committees. Other activities are meant to communicate with candidates: for example, direct contributions of cash or goods and services. Finally, some activities are meant to communicate with interest group members and voters at large: newsletters, voter mobilization efforts, Web pages, endorsements (and hit lists), independent expenditures, and issue advocacy campaigns.

Because the purposes of communication are often complex and the same communication may be directed to multiple audiences, not all electoral activity will fit this framework. For example, large corporations and labor unions may give soft money to parties in an effort to win favor with particular candidates; indeed, it is not uncommon for soft money to be unofficially directed to particular races (Jackson 1990). Yet soft money may also be used to remind the party that corporations and unions are an important part of a party's coalition. When an interest group makes independent expenditures to communicate with voters, such efforts may also signal to the candidate that the group strongly supports his or her candidacy. Similarly, voter mobilization comes under the heading of communicating with the electorate, but it also serves as an indication of an interest group's party loyalty and a reminder of its importance to the party coalition—measured by the number of voters the group is capable of delivering to the polls.

Recognizing that communication often has more than one purpose and more than one audience, we will structure our examination of interest groups around communication as a general theme. Chapter 2 focuses on the efforts of interest groups to influence the policy direction of political parties: recruiting and training candidates, sending delegations to party conventions, working to shape party platforms, and attempting to gain admission to the party apparatus. Chapter 3 describes the ways in which interest groups help candidates directly: by providing money, services, volunteers, and advice. Chapter 4 investigates interest groups' efforts to influence voters: by endorsing candidates or advocating their defeat, by undertaking independent expenditures and issue advocacy campaigns, and by attempting to mobilize their members and others to participate in politics. Each of these chapters begins by exploring the strategic context—the interaction of laws, regulations, and practices with interest groups' goals and resources—that shapes the selection of strategies and tactics. Each chapter then describes the specific activities of interest groups in detail. The concluding chapter evaluates the role of interest groups in electoral politics and considers a variety of proposals for reform.

NOTE

1. When this practice became public, the *Washington Post* mockingly dubbed the breakfasts "Eggs McBentsen." In the face of widespread criticism, the senator first defended the practice and then ended the breakfast meetings altogether.

CHAPTER 2

Interest Groups and Political Parties

In January 1998, the Republican National Committee (RNC) met in Indian Wells, California, to consider a resolution that would cut off party support for GOP candidates who did not oppose banning a late-term abortion procedure referred to by anti-abortion forces as "partial-birth abortion." Party chair Jim Nicholson, who had won his job in part because of Christian Coalition support, opposed the resolution, while GOP presidential hopeful Steve Forbes and Christian Coalition chair Randy Tate urged committee members to support it.

Although the resolution ultimately failed, it created a firestorm within the GOP and attracted national headlines for days. The debate over the resolution divided even social conservatives, some of whom urged support for the resolution on the basis of principle, while others—concerned about setting a precedent—argued that a national party should not apply a litmus test to identify candidates eligible for party support.

American parties in the past have witheld funding from candidates associated with extremist movements. In Louisiana, the GOP denied funding to David Duke, a former Ku Klux Klan member and leader of the American Nazi Party who had won the GOP gubernatorial primary; in Illinois, the Democratic Party withheld money from two followers of extremist Lyndon LaRouche who had won Democratic nominations for lieutenant governor and attorney general. During the 1994 House elections, GOP leaders tried to persuade Republican candidates to pledge their support for the Contract with America, a set of ten policies that party leaders promised to implement if they obtained a majority in that chamber. But the GOP controversy over late-term abortions was unprecedented: for the Republican Party even to consider withholding funding from candidates who failed to take a specific position on a divisive public issue is a vivid demonstration of the power of interest group politics in the internal life of American political parties.

Relationships between interest groups and political parties are complex and tend to vary with time and circumstance. In some cases, the connection is symbiotic, with both the party and the interest group benefiting; in other cases, relations can be tense, with occasional open conflict. In the 1990s, labor unions and the Democratic Party maintained a strong, mutually supportive link, with unions providing significant assistance to party candidates and performing many of the functions of the party itself, while the party supported labor on many important issues. Business groups had a similar relationship with the GOP: party leaders supported reductions in business taxes and in environmental, consumer, and safety regulations, while business groups provided money and services to the party.

Although relations between the civil rights movement and the Democrats and between the anti-abortion movement and the Republicans are generally supportive, they have been marked by occasional conflict. In the 1990s, civil rights groups pressured the Democratic Party to oppose welfare reform, threatening to bolt if Democrats moved too quickly to dismantle programs to assist low-income Americans. Similarly, in 1996, anti-abortion activists threatened to withdraw their support for the Republican ticket if Bob Dole selected a pro-choice running mate. In some states, moderate Republicans and the Christian right are engaged in virtual party warfare. In Virginia, in 1993 and 1994, moderate senator John Warner refused to endorse lieutenant governor nominee Michael Farris and openly opposed U.S. Senate nominee Oliver North—two candidates with strong backing from the Christian right. Christian conservatives retaliated by asking the Senate leadership to deny Warner the powerful position of chairman of the Rules Committee. On the floor of the 1993 Virginia convention, there was considerable pushing and shouting, and some Christian right delegates threw ice at some pro-choice speakers.

In Minnesota, relations between the Christian right and party regulars were similarly tense, but in other states—such as South Carolina and Georgia—Christian right groups formed a symbiotic relationship with the party (Bullock and Grant 1995; Bullock and Smith 1997; Gilbert and Peterson 1995, 1997; Guth 1995, 1997; Rozell and Wilcox 1996).

Chapter 1 noted that an interest group's choice of strategies and tactics depends on the interaction of two sets of factors: (1) the opportunity structures created by the political system, with its laws, regulations, and common practices, and (2) the goals and resources of the group. The interaction of the political system on the one hand and a group's goals and resources on the other creates the strategic context for interest group involvement in electoral activity. This chapter first describes the strategic context that leads some interest groups to communicate with, to influence the internal politics of, and in some cases even to "take over" political parties. The chapter then examines in some detail the varieties of tactics used to achieve such goals.

THE STRATEGIC CONTEXT: REGULATIONS, GOALS, AND RESOURCES

The Constitution does not even mention political parties, and few federal regulations affect them. In addition, the Supreme Court has ruled in recent years that the free speech rights of parties can be limited only to facilitate a "compelling state interest" in ensuring fair and orderly elections. For interest groups, much of the regulation that affects the opportunity structure comes from state governments. States retain considerable authority to regulate how political parties select their candidates and how they structure internal party committees; states may even regulate parties' internal rules and activities.

In all states, candidates are selected through some type of electoral process that allows voters to choose candidates. This process varies widely across states, across parties, and sometimes even within parties, primarily along two dimensions. First, states and parties choose among primary elections, caucuses, and conventions. Primary elections require little commitment from voters, other than showing up at the ballot box, and therefore generate higher turnout. Caucuses sometimes require voters to spend time in a public meeting and vote publicly, which helps explain why turnout is lower. State conventions are even more demanding, requiring that voters travel to the convention hall and sometimes dedicate the weekend to political activity. Because turnout is generally lower for caucuses and conventions than for primaries, it is much easier for interest groups to dominate caucuses and conventions than primary elections.

Second, state regulations determine who is allowed to vote in internal party elections. Some states restrict participation to voters who have registered a preference for a particular party (for example, only registered Democrats can vote in a Democratic primary). Other states allow independents to vote in either party's contest but forbid cross-party voting (for example, both registered Republicans and independents could vote in a Republican caucus). Still other states have open selection processes limiting voters to one internal election per year. Thus, any voters who wish to can attend the Democratic Party convention, but this would bar them from attending the GOP convention. Open rules for primary elections dilute the influence of interest groups, while open rules for conventions may actually strengthen their influence.

Compared with the political systems of other nations and with patterns prevalent earlier in U.S. history, however, all of these nomination procedures are unusually open to interest group involvement. In other Western democracies, party leaders select candidates, rewarding loyal party workers and promoting promising young party loyalists. A few interest groups with strong ties to a party may have some say in the nomination process, but in the United States, interest groups can independently recruit candidates and help them to win intraparty elections, even against candidates favored by party leaders.

States and parties determine the kinds of party committees that are allowed and the selection process for committee members. Both parties have national committees, state committees, and a variety of local committees (most commonly county committees and congressional district committees). Members of these committees are usually selected at open party meetings, which gives interest groups the opportunity to influence—and, on occasion, "take over"—party committees. If, for example, interest group members show up in large numbers, without warning, at a party meeting designed to elect the county party officers, they can sometimes ensure the election of their own activists to important posts, including party chair.

Unlike their counterparts in other Western democracies, American political parties are often deeply divided. In the 1960s and 1970s, the Democrats were divided between a progressive wing that included activists from civil rights, antiwar, and feminist groups and a moderate wing that included members of labor unions and business groups. In the 1990s, the

GOP has been split into a conservative wing that includes many members of Christian right groups and a moderate wing that includes many representatives of the business community. Such internal divisions may be more or less severe at times, but there is always debate about where the party should stand on economic, social, and foreign policy issues.

Disagreement within American parties provides an "opening" for interest group involvement and influence. In most other Western democracies, in contrast, political parties have enduring platforms that lay out the basic values and goals of the party and specify policies that the party will enact should it gain control of parliament. Party leaders determine which candidates will represent the party on the ballot, and all candidates are required to subscribe to the party platform and to pledge to support party legislation if they are elected. Candidates who do not pledge to vote the party line on all issues are routinely denied access to the ballot.

In the United States, although there are general ideological differences between the two major parties, candidates are free to adopt their own positions on all political issues. Within each party, contending factions vie to define the values that the party should support and the policies that it should pursue. They also struggle to influence the party platforms—which, in practice, often embody nothing more than the momentary sentiments of a majority of party activists.

Why would interest groups try to gain influence over political parties that cannot impose discipline on their members? First, by helping to determine which candidates receive party nominations, interest groups can indirectly influence who sits in Congress and the positions the party takes on crucial legislation. If a significant number of legislators are members or supporters of a particular interest group, they can often persuade their colleagues to pass or support legislation that enacts the policy preferences of that group; they can also try to obtain the support of their party caucus. The large number of Christian conservatives among GOP members of the House and Senate, for example, is one reason that Congress passed the "partial-birth abortion" ban in 1996. Similarly, the Congressional Black Caucus, a significant voting bloc among House Democrats, has on occasion swayed Democratic colleagues to support policies that aid cities or increase assistance for low-income citizens.

Second, by influencing the nomination process, interest group activists can pressure candidates to adopt particular positions. As anti-abortion activists moved into the Republican Party and pro-choice groups formed alliances with the Democrats, the abortion issue became a litmus test for presidential candidates, and pro-choice Republicans and anti-abortion Democrats were forced to change their public positions on the issue (Cook, Jelen, and Wilcox 1992). In the Republican Party, the strong presence of anti-abortion activists in the 1996 Republican nomination process is undoubtedly one of the reasons that businessman Steve Forbes—who had sought the GOP presidential nomination in 1996 as a social moderate—took an anti-abortion stance in 1997, as he began his second run for the presidency. Forbes's switch, in turn, echoed that of George Bush in 1980. Among Democrats, Al Gore, Richard Gephardt, and Jesse Jackson all moved to support a pro-choice position when they sought the presidency in the 1980s. As anti-abortion and pro-choice groups became active in recruiting and supporting candidates in party primaries, they succeeded in changing the composition of the parties' delegations to Congress and in creating genuine party differences on abortion at a time when the issue did not cleave the general public along partisan lines (Adams 1996).

Interest groups with broad public policy goals are most likely to work within political parties to nominate candidates and to influence party platforms. In general, these tactics are more likely to be used by social movement organizations, groups that succeed in mobilizing citizens previously outside of the party: for example, feminists and African Americans in the Democratic Party in the 1960s and 1970s and Christian conservatives in the Republican Party in the 1980s and 1990s. Yet even professional associations such as the National Association of Realtors (NAR) and the American Medical Association (AMA) become involved in internal party politics on occasion. Similarly, business groups played an important role in shaping the 1994 Republican Contract with America. Generally, however, groups with more narrow goals are more likely to approach incumbents directly than to work within political parties.

Although most interest group activity within parties is aimed at influencing public policy on controversial issues, at the national conventions corporations often find the occasion to cozy up to party leaders—helping, for example, to finance the convention, receptions, and other events; making large donations of soft money; and providing goods and services. The corporations are not seeking to influence party positions on controversial issues but are instead seeking access to policy makers who can help promote corporate economic interests.

One resource is central to effective intraparty electoral activity: membership. Social movement organizations have the best pool of resources: dedicated activists, a large membership base, and an even larger pool of sympathizers who might support movement candidates in primary elections. Interest groups with fewer members are less able to compete with other party factions.

RECRUITING AND TRAINING CANDIDATES

Candidate recruitment and training are important tactics in interest groups' efforts to achieve their policy goals. In American politics, citizens who want to run for office must declare their candidacy and are often required to assemble petitions before they can get their names on the ballot for a primary election or caucus. Although a number of potential candidates may consider running, most ultimately decide against mounting a campaign (Fowler and McClure 1989). By reaching out to potential candidates and offering encouragement and support, interest groups can influence who decides to run. By offering training, interest groups can influence who wins.

Approaches to Recruitment

Many interest groups find that the most reliable and loyal candidates can be drawn from the activist and leadership bases of their own organizations. To date, however, only a few interest groups have recruited candidates from within their ranks, and these candidates have constituted only a small percentage of all candidates in congressional elections. But there is evidence that this pattern may be changing: feminist and Christian right groups are increasing their efforts to recruit members to run for office, and the AFL-CIO has begun to aggressively encourage union members to seek public office. In late 1997, federation president John Sweeney announced the "Goals 2000" initiative—a plan to actively recruit at least two thousand labor unionists to run for public office by the year 2000. Under Sweeney's leadership, the federation decided that it could best promote its goals by recruiting its own members rather than by recruiting and training candidates outside the movement who may agree with some—but not all—of the labor agenda. Although most of the AFL-CIO's efforts focus on local offices, long-term gains are potentially substantial, including not only more policies that are sympathetic to labor but also a pool of strong candidates for federal office.

Although interest groups may look first to their own members, many recruit nonmembers as well, identifying individuals with good political skills who appear to share their policy goals and encouraging them to seek higher office. Interest groups interested in recruiting candidates for the U.S. House usually begin by encouraging citizens to run for local or state office—city council, county commission, or state legislature. Because many candidates for the House first serve in local government, interest groups have ample opportunity to work closely with many members of the candidate pool and assess their support for the group's priorities.

Recruitment is especially important for interest groups that wish to increase the number of policy makers from previously underrepresented groups, such as women, racial and ethnic minorities, and Christian conservatives. Without the encouragement and assistance of interest groups, many talented citizens who are members of such demographic groups would not otherwise consider running for political office; interest groups thus play an important role in increasing the diversity of demographic representation among officeholders.

The National Women's Political Caucus (NWPC) has mounted a large coordinated effort to recruit women to run for public office. In 1994, the caucus began a series of training events to teach state and local activists how to identify candidates and campaign managers, generally for state legislative and county offices but also for House and Senate seats. Democratic pollster Celinda Lake advised the caucus to seek out women who have their own businesses, who are important members of community organizations, or who serve on local school boards or other appointed or elected bodies. In a number of states, the caucus has mounted sophisticated efforts, first determining which state legislative and congressional districts might be open seats (where new candidates stand the best chance of winning), then identifying potential women candidates to run for those offices (Duerst-Lahti 1998). According to Heather Herndon, political director of the NWPC, members often call her about potential candidates, saying "there's this woman who would be perfect." Herndon follows up by calling the woman, talking to her, getting her into a training program, and offering encouragement. Then there are those, Herndon notes, who "self-select"—who call her themselves and tell her that they want to run.

The NWPC has state and local caucuses throughout the country, and recruitment is most likely to occur when activists identify potential candidates in their own communities. The national organization facilitates the recruitment process by providing local caucuses with a recruitment manual. According to Herndon, the manual provides information such as "how to find candidates, how to approach them, how to actually recruit them."

The manual tells recruiters how to find women candidates who fit the profile of the district, provides guidelines on how to take candidates through the process, and offers tips on how to help candidates overcome any fears that they may have about running. In addition, the manual covers the technicalities that might seem overwhelming to a new candidate, such as how to get started and how to file.

For caucus leaders, the manual provides advice on how to instruct candidates on a number of other aspects of campaigning—researching the district, assessing opponents, identifying sympathetic interest groups, conducting media interviews, and fund raising (National Women's Political Caucus 1997b).

The National Rifle Association (NRA) also relies on local activists to recruit candidates. According to Tanya Metaksa, executive director of the NRA Institute for Legislative Affairs, the NRA has "a lot of members who are interested in promoting other members of the organization for public office." Metaksa notes that recruitment efforts do not "just come out of national headquarters" but take place throughout the country. NRA members are "active in many ways, including trying to identify people who might run for office and trying to educate them on our positions on the issues."

Civil rights organizations have played an active role in recruiting black candidates. Within the African American community, churches have historically recruited and trained candidates for all levels of public office, providing them with opportunities to develop leadership and organizational skills, to cultivate a constituency of supporters, and to emerge as activists and leaders. Even today, many black elected officials are ministers who periodically return to their districts to preach to a congregation.

Similarly, Christian conservative organizations recruit activists who have developed their political skills in white evangelical churches. The Christian right has been quite active in encouraging Christian conservatives to run for county office, for school boards, and even for Congress. Christian right groups provide training sessions on campaign mechanics (how to form a campaign committee, how to set up a campaign account) as well as on matters of presentation (how to address such issues as abortion and health care).

Although many organizations are eager to increase the number of elected officials who fit a particular demographic profile, most will support only those candidates who favor a specific policy agenda and have a credible chance of winning. At the NWPC, for example, candidate recruitment and training are clearly a means toward achieving policy ends. Candidates seeking campaign assistance must favor abortion rights, the equal rights amendment (ERA), and child and dependent care. According to Heather Herndon, a strong candidate who is "right" on only two out of these three issues will not be supported by the caucus.

Although agreement on policy may be the first and most important criterion for recruitment, it is not necessarily enough: interest groups want candidates who are electable. For example, the leadership manual of the Christian Coalition, the nation's largest Christian right organization, asks, "What kind of people make the best candidates for public office, and where do you find them?" The manual then notes that although surface impressions—"poise, good looks, brains"—are not irrelevant, they can be misleading. Christian right leaders are advised to also take the following into account: background; achievement; other personal characteristics, such as the ability to balance the ticket; and competence for office.

Despite the fact that competence for office is the last criterion listed, the organization does encourage Christian right leaders to assess whether a candidate can win before beginning the recruitment process. Thus, under the topic of "personal background," the manual notes that recruitment involves the "unpleasant task" of "digging out . . . intimate details"—including whether a potential candidate has a bad credit rating, a poor professional reputation, questionable moral character, or an unpublicized divorce. The Christian Coalition wants its leaders to recruit viable candidates who will do a good job in office; but, like other groups, it first wants potential candidates to demonstrate commitment to the movement's values (Fisher, Reed, and Weinhold 1990).

Recruitment by interest groups is usually most important for state and local office and to a lesser extent for the U.S. House. Most senatorial and presidential races involve ambitious and established politicians who have long considered making a bid for higher office. Yet even here, recruitment efforts can be important. A potential candidate may be mulling over a race for the Senate or the presidency, weighing the costs in time, money, and wear and tear on family life, and commitments of support from interest groups may help determine whether—and for what office—the candidate runs. Upon occasion, interest group activists do run for higher office. In 1988, Pat Robertson and Jesse Jackson, two ordained Baptist ministers who represented the Christian right and the civil rights movement, respectively, sought the presidency; in late 1998, Gary Bauer, another leading Christian right activist, was considering a presidential bid. In other cases, interest groups actively encourage candidates to run; in 1998, labor unions were urging Richard Gephardt to seek the presidency, while environmental groups were reassuring Al Gore of their continued support.

Training Methods

Once they have identified and encouraged good candidates to enter a campaign, interest groups provide various forms of training: seminars, manuals, and video and audio tapes, along with other sources of advice. Training is most common for U.S. House and state legislative races; few candidates for the Senate or the presidency believe that they need training to improve their candidacy, although a few could probably use some advice. Political parties and quasi-party organizations also offer training to candidates, and interest groups often refer candidates they have recruited to party-run training sessions.

Interest groups that offer training vary in their approaches; some are content to mail helpful materials to candidates, whereas others send staff throughout the country to conduct training seminars. Training focuses on two principal concerns:(1) issues presentation, the art of framing issues in a way that is favorable to the interest group; and (2) campaign techniques, the basic tasks of running a campaign.

The NRA focuses on issues presentation. To assist sympathetic candidates in framing issues, the group mails out a multimedia package entitled *The Politics of Crime: Winning Strategies for Your Campaign* (National Rifle Association 1994). The centerpiece of the package is a video, introduced by Tanya Metaksa as a short course in how to respond to gun control advocates and how to develop a winning campaign message on crime and guns. The opening sequence is a frightening re-creation of an actual 911 emergency call in which a woman with a baby pleads for help as a violent criminal breaks into her house, then into her locked bedroom. Authorities are unable to come to the rescue in time, and the message is clear: with a gun, the woman could have protected herself and her child; without one, she was vulnerable. The video then features a sequence that includes expert testimony, campaign ads, speeches, and statements from crime victims. A closing comment by Metaksa emphasizes that candidates must not only have the right positions on gun rights issues but must also adhere to those positions consistently throughout the campaign.

In addition, the NRA training package contains an audiotape version of *The Politics of Crime,* an NRA report on criminal justice reform, a booklet to supplement the video and audio tapes, and reprints of articles from journals and popular magazines. The reprinted articles emphasize, first, that gun control does not work, and second, that taking a tough position on crime is good politics. The overall goal of the materials is to convince candidates that adopting the NRA view will put them on the winning side—as long as they carefully control the message by focusing on crime, not gun control. Metaksa notes: "We focus on the areas of crime and firearms, not so much on the mechanics of running a campaign and doing fund raising. We focus on the policy arena: how to frame the debate." Metaksa goes on to observe that whoever "grasps the message first and does it well will end up forcing his or her opponent" to take a defensive position. The summary of the glossy publication *The Politics of Crime* makes this same point: to run a successful campaign in favor of gun rights, candidates must keep the focus not on guns, but on crime, which is where their opponents are vulnerable (see Box 2-1).

Like the NRA, the National Federation of Independent Businesses (NFIB) uses a packet of educational materials to focus on issues presentation. The centerpiece of NFIB training is a video of sample campaign advertisements. The intent is to show candidates how to present a pro–small business message in a campaign and to convince them that such a message is a formula for success. The video presentation is backed up by corroborating printed materials. Political director Jeff Butsky also invites prospective candidates to visit the NFIB for one-on-one interviews to "talk about small-business issues and how to incorporate them into a campaign."

> We will then mail out a letter to our members in that district asking them to volunteer their time with that candidate. Then we have regional political directors and they go out and meet with our members and instruct the members on how to become involved politically. The members then develop liaisons with the candidate informing him or her of their concerns on small-business issues and in turn offering their volunteer services to the campaign.

In addition to distributing multimedia educational materials, other interest groups provide formal training in campaign techniques. The NWPC holds about ten training schools for candidates each year, in conjunction with the organization's regional caucus meetings. According to Heather Herndon, "The local caucuses do the real recruiting of candidates, and we do the on-site training for them: we provide the trainers, the manuals, and the other materials."

BOX 2-1

FROM *THE POLITICS OF CRIME*

Violent crime is one of the single most important issues in America today. It will be a key factor in virtually every campaign in 1994.

Members of the media and "liberal scholars" are telling us that guns, not criminals, are the problem. Big guns, small guns, ugly guns, whatever. And they're telling us that the answer is to ban them, tax them, register them, control them. Some of them, all of them, you name it. But gun control doesn't reduce crime. It never has and it never will. The statistics prove it and the public knows it.

The real issue is crime control, not gun control, and there are votes for candidates who are willing to be tough on crime, tough on criminals, and who propose workable, long-term solutions. To make this issue work for your campaign, you must stake out a position early and clearly; make the commitment of resources necessary to communicate your position; organize your supporters; and work to keep the anti-gun, pro-criminal lobby on the defensive, discussing crime on *your terms,* not theirs.

Source: Excerpted from National Rifle Association, "Summary," *The Politics of Crime: Winning Strategies for Your Campaign* (Fairfax, Va.: National Rifle Association, 1994), 11. Used with permission of the National Rifle Association of America Institute for Legislative Action.

The NWPC gives its candidates and campaign workers a training manual entitled *Campaigning to Win: The NWPC Guide to Running a Winning Campaign* (National Women's Political Caucus 1997a). The highly detailed manual covers, among other topics, hiring campaign staff and structuring a campaign organization; budgeting and fund raising; developing a public image; targeting and contacting voters; and dealing with the media. Some of the advice is quite specific; sections with titles such as "TV Clothing Tips" and "Special Speaking Tips for Women Candidates" include advice such as the following:

Always have an extra pair of nylons handy in case of runs. On a hot day, a candidate may want to take along an extra blouse as well. Some candidates prepare for the unexpected by leaving a spare set of clothes at campaign headquarters or in the car.

The manual explains that because of a societal double standard, women are more likely to be judged on the basis of appearance than men. In addition to offering candidates guidance on what colors and patterns to wear and what fabrics to avoid, the manual advises them not to change their hairstyle or the design of their eyeglasses during a campaign, not to wear "bold earrings" or too much makeup, and to dress in business attire but to "avoid wearing designer outfits that cost more than the average voter's monthly salary." In a series of detailed tips on television "body language," the manual explains the importance of looking animated rather than too serious, describes how to make eye contact with the news anchor or reporter, and offers guidelines on the use of hand gestures: "Keep all gestures within an imaginary box the size of a twenty-one-inch television screen from your chin down to your chest, between the shoulder blades, and six to eight inches out" (National Women's Political Caucus 1997a) (see Box 2-2).

The level and type of instruction are keyed to the candidates' backgrounds and interests. For example, the NWPC offers an advanced training program for incumbents looking to move to higher positions and for field workers seeking to learn campaign management. The training seminars open with general sessions for all participants, then the candidates and campaign workers split up to focus on their particular needs.

EMILY's List (Early Money Is Like Yeast) also offers a combination of training materials and seminars. The training schools cover both issues and strategies, addressing topics such as how to handle discussions about women's issues, how to do media interviews, and how to create campaign ads. As deputy trainer Mitchel Lester explains, EMILY's List will arrange for a media trainer to come in and talk to the candidates about how to present themselves on camera; then the candidates will have a trial run, and the trainer will explain what they did right and what they did wrong.

Candidate training seminars are most common among organizations recruiting candidates who may lack certain political skills—especially feminist groups, civil rights groups, and Christian conservative groups. The business community does not offer training seminars, although the National Association of Realtors (NAR), for example, used to conduct candidate training schools and provide its preferred candidates with a training manual (National Association of Realtors 1991). The NAR manual covered topics similar to those covered by the training publications of other inter-

BOX 2-2

SPECIAL SPEAKING TIPS FOR WOMEN CANDIDATES

Candidates must have a strong ego, but many women are afraid to blow their own horn. Go ahead and brag about your strong points.

Control your emotions, especially anger or tears. Avoid tilting your head or using other body language which suggests a lack of confidence.

Recognize that some voters question a woman's leadership skills. Highlight any experience that shows you leading others or making tough decisions.

Be prepared to speak on all issues that the winner will have to face. Some voters still link female candidates only with "family" issues such as health care and education.

Voters may pay more attention to your family status than that of your male opponent(s). If you're single, be prepared for curiosity about your sex life or speculation about your sexual preference. You may want to find an appropriate escort for some events. If you have children, find a good, reliable baby-sitter, preferably a relative.

Prepare answers for stupid questions. For example, "What does your husband think about your candidacy?" Possible response: "He supports me and recognizes that my background and work in our community make me the best candidate for this office."

Avoid drinking alcohol or smoking cigarettes in public.

Source: Excerpted from "Special Speaking Tips for Women Candidates," National Women's Political Caucus (NWPC), *Campaigning to Win: The NWPC Guide to Running a Winning Campaign* (Washington, D.C.: NWPC, 1994), 7–10. Used with permission.

est groups, such as campaign planning, publicity, precinct targeting, and debate tactics. The NAR manual was very specific on some matters—for example, how to avoid having campaign buttons end up mostly in the hands of political memorabilia collectors and what information is appropriate to include in billboard advertisements (see Box 2-3).

The NAR decided to abandon its candidate training, however, when such efforts were superceded by the growth of the party campaign school.

BOX 2-3

CAMPAIGN ADVICE FROM THE
NATIONAL ASSOCIATION OF REALTORS

If your message fails to move voters, find one that moves them. The worst campaign is the one that is still searching for a theme right up to election day. That is why research and targeting of voter groups at the earliest stage of a campaign is vital to your campaign's ultimate success. . . . Advertising agencies can be very helpful to you in sharpening your theme and message. Depending on time and budget, these firms can help you focus your message and reduce it to two or three key areas that will move voters. Moving voters is what a campaign is about.

Posters should be designed in an attractive manner, and . . . fit the theme of the campaign. The name copy should be clear, the message sharp. If a photograph of the candidate is used, be sure to use one that is flattering and current.

Billboards also add to name recognition and a sense of momentum in a campaign. A handful of properly placed billboards can be more effective than numerous billboards placed in non-productive areas. . . . Billboards should be well-lighted for night viewing, and high above ground clutter or other distractions or competitive impressions.

A secondary button that has gained popularity over the years is the cloth type with the sticky back. They are much less expensive and easy to hand out, do not puncture skin, do not stick holes in cloth, and are excellent for application to notebooks, pads, brief cases and purses. Another button that is less expensive is the thin metal button with a fold down clip that can slip into a pocket or in a button hole. Campaign buttons should be very simple with only your name identification and the office you seek (and perhaps the year). Pictures on a button increase the production costs and use valuable space. Voters cast votes by name, not by pictures.

Source: Excerpted from National Association of Realtors (NAR), *Getting There: Becoming a Realtor Public Official* (Washington, D.C.: NAR, 1991).

NAR political director Trey Richardson notes that the party organizations "can do it a lot better than any group since they have the more immediate access to the best campaign people, pollsters, elected officials and others who do the best training." One of the most prominent party-related groups conducting candidate training is Rep. Newt Gingrich's GOPAC. Although not officially a part of the formal party structure, GOPAC exclusively promotes the fortunes of conservative Republican candidates at all levels. If a GOP candidate sympathetic to the NAR approached Richardson about campaign advice, he might put her in touch with GOPAC staff, who would then provide the candidate with the necessary training.

Like some of the groups discussed earlier in this section, GOPAC offers candidates both training seminars and a multimedia package, but several of its training services go far beyond those offered by groups that are focused on specific issues. According to Peter Roff, the organization's political director, GOPAC has five different training programs, each geared toward a particular purpose, and a number of GOPAC trainers travel throughout the country conducting seminars. The program for elected legislators teaches them how to use their incumbency for future electoral advantage. Another program teaches candidates how to communicate effectively in different contexts—speeches, debates, media interviews, television advertisements. Another program focuses on campaign strategies and tactics, yet another on fund raising. Finally, GOPAC offers financially strapped challengers a seminar on how to run a grassroots, volunteer-based campaign.

Other conservative groups often request permission to review and adapt GOPAC's training materials for their own purposes. Even unsympathetic groups have learned from the opposing forces: EMILY's List seeks to emulate some of the tactics mastered by GOPAC, and a state Democratic legislative caucus director acknowledged that in developing training booklets for candidates and activists, he borrowed freely from the Christian Coalition's training manual, which he believed to be the most sophisticated at that time (Rozell and Wilcox 1996, 85).

THE NOMINATION PROCESS

In addition to recruiting and training candidates, a number of interest groups provide direct assistance to candidates seeking their party's nomination. Interest groups may endorse candidates, provide voters' guides to their members and other voters, contribute money or services directly to the candidate, engage in voter mobilization efforts, and even pay for television advertising.

Again, such tactics are most common among social movement organizations. Feminist, civil rights, and Christian right groups all support candidates in primaries, sometimes marshaling significant resources on their behalf. Such groups can play an important role in determining party nominations, especially in states that nominate through conventions or caucuses rather than through primaries.

As noted earlier, turnout is lower in states with caucuses or conventions, enabling a well-organized and dedicated minority of voters to significantly influence party nominations. Nevertheless, interest groups can play an important role even in primary elections. In Kansas in 1996, interest groups poured millions of dollars into a party primary pitting Sheila Frahm, a moderate state legislator appointed by the governor to fill Bob Dole's seat until the fall election, against Congressman Sam Brownback, a social conservative. Both candidates raised money from corporate committees, but pro-choice and women's groups helped Frahm, while anti-abortion and other conservative groups rallied behind Brownback, who won the nomination (Cigler and Loomis 1997). Table 2-1 shows some of the ideological and partisan PACs that contributed money in that primary.

Contributions to candidates, endorsements, voter mobilization, and other interest group tactics will be discussed in more detail in Chapters 3 and 4. For now it is important to understand that groups use their resources to try to influence party nomination politics. Groups that mount sustained, national efforts to influence party nominations have the opportunity to influence the policies that the party espouses.

PRESIDENTIAL NOMINATIONS

Of course, many interest groups focus their greatest efforts on influencing presidential nominations. Because the positions of candidates within the same party often differ greatly, interest groups may have much at stake. Consider, for example, GOP candidates Pat Buchanan and Steve Forbes, who finished second and third, after Bob Dole, for the 1996 GOP presidential nomination. Buchanan criticized big business for shipping American jobs overseas and for marketing products without regard to their impact on American culture, favored protection for American products,

TABLE 2-1

PAC Contributions to Candidates in the 1996 Kansas Senate Primary

Contributions to Sam Brownback

Campaign America	$1,000
Citizens Allied for Free Enterprise	1,000
National Right to Life PAC	2,000
Maryland Association for Concerned Citizens PAC	3,000
Conservative Victory Committee	3,500
Eagle Forum PAC	4,000
American Free Enterprise PAC	4,500
Free Congress PAC	4,670
Citizens United Political Victory Fund	5,000
Conservative Campaign Fund	5,000
Faith Family & Freedom PAC	5,000
The Madison Project, Inc., Fund	5,000
Republican National Coalition for Life PAC	5,000
Total	$48,670

Contributions to Sheila Frahm

Republican Primary PAC	$500
The Capitol Committee	1,000
Modern Political Action Committee	1,000
Republicans for Choice	1,000
WISH List	4,907
Committee for Responsible Government	5,000
Minnesota Women's Campaign Fund	5,000
Senate Victory Fund PAC	5,000
Total	$23,407

Source: Compiled from Federal Election Commission data.

and argued that immigration diluted the American character. On social issues, Buchanan took a strong stance against abortion and gay rights. Forbes defended big business and supported tax breaks that would aid the most affluent, favored free trade, did not oppose immigration, and argued (in 1996) that abortion was primarily a private matter. With two candidates at odds on so many important issues, the party nomination could hardly be a matter of inconsequence.

In 1996, both the Democratic and GOP conventions were carefully stage-managed affairs in which the nominees—who were not in doubt—controlled the message, if not always the platform. Yet it is important to understand that the rules for selecting nominees have changed over time, with important implications for interest group participation. Moreover, parties are free to change the rules for presidential nominations in the future, and the rules are not neutral in their effect: whatever form they take, they create part of the opportunity structure for interest groups that wish to influence internal party affairs.

In the 1968 Democratic National Convention, despite deep internal dissent over civil rights and the Vietnam War, party rules allowed an elite group to award the nomination to Vice President Hubert H. Humphrey, who had not entered a single state primary or caucus. Senators Eugene McCarthy and George McGovern had run in a number of state primaries and caucuses, but these same rules made it impossible for these populist antiwar candidates to prevail. In frustration over the nomination and in protest against the Johnson-Humphrey administration's policies on Vietnam, thousands of activists took to the streets outside the convention while others remained in the hall, repeatedly disrupting the proceedings.

Four years later, George McGovern won the party's presidential nomination by successfully defeating his opponents in a lengthy series of open primary contests that chose delegates to the national convention. What made McGovern's victory possible was a fundamental change in party rules governing nominations. In 1969, McGovern had helped direct a reform commission that proposed dramatic changes in the nominating process—changes that the party ultimately adopted. That McGovern himself benefited from the new rules was no coincidence: he understood that the traditional leaders of the party would never turn to him as a presidential nominee and that a populist candidacy such as his would fare best under an open primary process.

In 1972, twenty-three states held Democratic presidential primaries—six more than in 1968—and almost 61 percent of convention delegates were selected by primary election (including a huge block of 271 delegates from California, which McGovern won narrowly in 1972). Under a complex formula, the composition of the convention delegates reflected the actual percentages in the population of women, minorities, and even young people (eighteen to twenty-one years of age) who had been given the right to vote for the first time. With its presidential nominee selected by the most open, participatory process in U.S. history and the most broadly diverse and "representative" group of delegates ever, the Democratic Party lost the election in a landslide of equally historic proportions.

By 1976, with further changes in the rules, thirty presidential primaries selected 73 percent of delegates to the Democratic conventions; but more important, party rules were changed to prohibit "winner-take-all" primaries, in which the winning candidate receives all the delegates: instead, candidates received delegates in rough proportion to their strength in the primary.

The Republican Party also opened its nomination process during the early 1970s, although it added fewer primaries and retained winner-take-all rules. Both parties have continued to change the nomination process during the past several decades; indeed, the Democratic Party makes minor modifications after almost every election cycle. But since 1972, both parties' nominations have been determined through a system of state primaries and caucuses over a period of several months.

Changes in rules governing nominations have profoundly affected interest group participation in conventions. Under the old rules, convention delegates were chosen at state conventions and caucuses where party insiders ran the show. This system favored groups with long-established ties to party elites (for example, labor unions and the Democratic Party, business interests and the GOP). Under more open nominating systems, delegates are allotted according to the popular vote. Interest groups that successfully mobilize activists in primary elections and caucuses can thus play an important role in nominations, including sending members as delegates to the nominating conventions.

In the 1968 Democratic convention, interest groups with close party ties influenced the nomination, while activists from ideological groups demonstrated outside the convention hall. In 1972, under a different set of rules, grassroots activists dominated the selection of the party standard-bearer, while some representatives of established interests failed to be selected as delegates. (Outside the convention hall, future Speaker of the House Thomas P. O'Neil quipped that he had been defeated for a slot as a party delegate by "the cast of *Hair.*") By 1996, with neither nomination in doubt, interest groups at the Democratic and Republican conventions focused their efforts on platforms and party rules, buying access to party leaders by donating large amounts of soft money to the party and by sponsoring hospitality suites, parties, and other events. Some groups used the media to communicate directly with the public, and others even staged protests.

Modern national conventions formally nominate presidential candidates. The nominees are chosen by delegates who are in turn selected at state party primaries and caucuses leading up to the conventions. The parties have complex and sometimes changing formulas for allocating delegates to each state. In general, however, both Democrats and Republicans award extra delegates to states that have supported the party's nominee in recent presidential elections; the GOP also favors less populous states (Wayne 1996).

The number of delegates from a state who support each candidate is based on the popular primary or caucus votes. Each party has a different formula for determining the precise number of delegates for each candidate, but in general, the Democrats assign delegates on the basis of the percentage vote for each candidate (with a bonus for the primary or caucus winner), and the Republicans have a winner-take-all system in which the candidate with the most votes gets all the delegates from a state. In the Democrats' modified proportional system, somewhat smaller groups that might be shut out in a winner-take-all system have the opportunity to send delegates to conventions and to have a voice in the proceedings. The Democrats also have a special category of "superdelegates"—elected officials, members of the party national committee, and other party leaders. But the vast majority of delegates are pledged to vote for the winner of a primary election or caucus in their state or district.

Studies show that participation rates in party primaries and caucuses are relatively low and that those who do participate are unrepresentative of voters in general elections (Ceaser 1979, 1982; Ladd 1978). Interest groups that can mobilize their members can thus have a strong influence on primary elections and especially on caucuses. Consider, for example, the success of Pat Robertson, a Christian conservative candidate who ran for the GOP nomination in 1988, and Jesse Jackson, an African American civil rights leader who sought the Democratic nomination in 1984 and 1988. Christian conservatives and African Americans each constitute between 10 and 20 percent of the general public, but if members of either group turn out in force to vote in a primary or caucus, their strength is significantly increased. In the Iowa caucuses, Robertson finished ahead of then–vice president George Bush simply because Robertson's supporters turned out to vote. (Bush joked lamely that his supporters had all been at their daughters' debutante balls on caucus night.) In 1988, civil rights groups and black churches helped Jesse Jackson win several primary states in the South.

Indeed, because participants in caucuses and some party primaries disproportionately represent interest groups, many scholars argue that the current presidential nomination process is heavily skewed in favor of ideological and issue-oriented candidates capable of appealing to interest group activists (Banfield 1980; Ceaser 1979, 1982; Ladd 1978; Wilson 1962). Nevertheless, party moderates often defeat more extreme candidates: both George Bush and Bob Dole defeated Patrick Buchanan for the GOP nomination in 1992 and 1996, and Bill Clinton defeated Jesse Jackson and Paul Simon in 1992.

Ideological groups do not, in fact, always support ideological candidates. Many conservative groups supported Dole in 1996 because they believed that he was more electable than Buchanan—and, perhaps more important, because they thought that Buchanan might do so badly in a presidential election that a Democrat-controlled Congress would ride in on Clinton's coattails. Christian Coalition executive director Ralph Reed worked behind the scenes to improve Bob Dole's chances with Christian conservative voters. Many analysts credit Reed for Dole's crucial victory in the South Carolina primary, which was achieved in large part with Christian right support. Elizabeth Drew reported that the day after Buchanan's New Hampshire victory, leaders of various influential conservative groups met to discuss what they could do to help stop Buchanan's momentum and enable the party to retain control of Congress (Drew 1997, 1).

DELEGATE SELECTION

Once primary elections and caucuses have been held, delegates are pledged by state law and party rules to support the winning candidates. Yet the actual selection of convention delegates occurs later, often in a series of local caucuses and regional conventions that sometimes culminate in a state convention. Many interest groups encourage their members to participate in the selection of delegates and try to send large blocs of their members to national conventions. Some interest group blocs actually meet together during the convention, and a few even have sophisticated "whip" systems to help deliver the votes on party platforms and rules (Schlozman and Tierney 1986).

In the GOP, although delegates from a state are all pledged to vote for the candidate who received the most votes in that state, not all the delegates necessarily support that candidate. Historically, winning candidates have dominated the delegate selection process, although they have often allowed the strongest supporters of losing candidates to serve as delegates to the national convention. In 1988, however, Pat Robertson contested the delegate selection process in states where he had lost primary elections, and members of conservative Christian groups sent many more delegates to the convention than they might have otherwise. In Virginia, for example, Robertson's supporters, who were mostly members of conservative Christian groups, worked hard (at local caucuses, congressional district conventions, and the state convention) to get selected as delegates to the national convention. Eventually, a majority of Virginia's delegates were Robertson supporters who were pledged to support Bush at the convention. By ensuring that a majority of delegates were Robertson supporters, the Christian right gained control of the Republican party apparatus in Virginia (Rozell and Wilcox 1996). A similar approach was used in other states as well (Herztke 1993).

Interest groups often send substantial delegations to the parties' national conventions. In 1984, Walter Mondale had 2,076 pledged delegates at the San Francisco convention, of whom 563 were members of unions of the AFL-CIO, 220 were members of the National Education Association (NEA), and 280 were members of the National Organization for Women (Schlozman and Tierney 1986). In 1996, 28 percent of the delegates to the Democratic National Convention were members of either the AFL-CIO or the NEA (Sack 1996a), and over 1,000 Democratic convention delegates overall were labor union members, of whom 405 delegates and alternates were NEA members (Wolf 1996).

In 1996, the Christian Coalition spent over $2 million to get its members and sympathizers elected as delegates to the Republican National Convention (Jackson 1996b). The effort paid off: about five hundred delegates—one out of every four—were registered members of the Christian Coalition, and two-thirds of all delegates were either members or supporters. The group then spent an additional $750,000 at the convention itself. In all, expenditures came to about $6,000 per member or supporter elected as a GOP delegate—a good measure of the importance that some groups attach to convention politics.

Occasionally, the selection of delegates to the presidential convention sparks visible and divisive fights within state parties. In Texas in 1996, many delegates on the slate proposed by the Dole campaign were defeated in the congressional district caucuses, including former party chair Fred Meyer, U.S. House members Henry Bonilla and Mac Thornberry, and the co-chair of Dole's Texas campaign. The greatest controversy surrounded the defeat of U.S. senator Kay Bailey Hutchison, who was later seated as an at-large delegate after the intervention of the governor, the party chair, Sen. Dole, and Sen. Phil Gramm (Bruce 1997).

THE NATIONAL CONVENTIONS

Why do groups such as labor unions and Christian conservatives work so hard to send delegates to the parties' national conventions? First, a strong and visible presence at a national convention signals to party leaders that an interest group is an important constituency that cannot be ignored in policy making. Second, conventions ratify the party platform, which embodies the official policy preferences of the party. Third, rules for delegate selection may be altered at conventions, which may affect candidates' chances in the next election. At the 1988 Democratic convention, Jesse Jackson's delegates successfully pressured the party to make its rules more favorable to "outsider" candidates. In addition, conventions provide interest group members with the opportunity to rub shoulders with party leaders and elected officials, perhaps doing a bit of unofficial lobbying in the process. And perhaps most important, group members who attend national conventions are often inspired to become more active, not only within their own interest group but also in the broader realm of electoral politics.

Conventions also provide interest groups with an opportunity to publicize their issues, inviting speakers and using the media to reach delegates and the larger electorate. In 1996, the labor union delegates' caucus sponsored numerous meetings and receptions, including one that featured speeches by Vice President Al Gore and Labor Secretary Robert Reich. On the opening day of the convention, the AFL–CIO sponsored a public rally to promote its "America Needs a Raise" campaign (Sack 1996b; Wolf 1996). Because television broadcasts of the conventions draw large numbers of viewers and convention halls are filled with reporters looking for a story, rallies and presentations can help publicize and promote interest groups' positions on crucial issues.

Many interest groups also use conventions as an opportunity to protest party policies. Before the 1996 Democratic convention, the city of Chicago held a lottery to award one-hour time slots to groups that wanted to stage protests outside the convention hall, designating two areas for protests and even providing the speaker system for the protesters (to regulate the noise level). The primary purpose of the lottery was to limit the number of groups staging protests and to ensure that the pandemonium of 1968 would not be repeated. Among the varied groups that applied for the right to protest were physicians angry at the lack of national health coverage, the Cuban-American Chamber of Commerce, the National Alliance Against Racism, White America United, the Yippies, and the Not on the Guest List Coalition (Terry 1996).

The calendar of official events at the 1996 GOP convention in San Diego included the following: a gathering at St. Paul's Episcopal Cathedral sponsored by the Religious Coalition for Reproductive Choice; a "Whale of a Party" at Sea World sponsored by the Republican National Coalition for Life; a "Military Salute to Senator Dole" sponsored by the Veterans Coalition; Charlton Heston's Arena PAC Kick-Off at the Planet Hollywood restaurant; and the Chrysler/RNC Family Day–Automobile Exhibit in downtown San Diego (Master Calendar of Events 1996).

Two of the largest group gatherings drew attention to the abortion issue. Outside the convention hall, seventy-five protesters from Operation Rescue held a rally. Angry at the GOP's apparent willingness to downplay anti-abortion politics out of political expediency, the group called attention to its cause by displaying a small coffin with an aborted fetus inside and inviting members of the news media to photograph the exhibit. The Christian Coalition held a convention-sponsored outdoor rally attended by two thousand supporters and including appearances by such leading Republicans as vice presidential nominee Jack Kemp, former vice president Dan Quayle, Governors Steve Merrill of New Hampshire and David Beasley of South Carolina, House Speaker Newt Gingrich, and Rep. J. C. Watts of Oklahoma. Although this event was more "mainstream" than the Operation Rescue rally, it also featured attention-grabbing graphic displays, including large signs with photographs of aborted fetuses (Clines 1996).

Inside the convention hall, some interest groups try to coordinate the actions of their members. At the 1996 GOP convention, the Christian Coalition made what was perhaps the most extensive coordination effort by any group in history. The group had 102 whips, 8 regional whips, 40 runners on the convention floor, and a war room to map out strategy. Perhaps most important, it provided each of its delegates with a new digital communications system—in essence, hand-held computers—using a new wireless frequency that had just been approved by the Federal Communications Commission. According to Christian Coalition executive director Ralph Reed, the communication system would afford his group a tremendous advantage in any potential floor debate and would also enable him, for example, to signal to delegates when to cheer during speeches (Drew 1997, 120; Goldberg 1996a; Jackson 1996b). The *New York Times* described how the Christian Coalition used the new technology to create the most efficient whip system at the convention:

> When an important vote is coming up, the whips will try to tally who will vote and how they will vote by canvassing delegates in advance at their hotels, but they will also do it quickly on the floor. When the whips have an accurate tally they will send it with a runner to one of 15 communications hubs on the floor, where it will be punched into the handheld computer and sent to the war room.
>
> In that room, . . . strategists with tally sheets, personal computers and more conventional tools of political battle will assess their strength.
>
> After deciding what tactic to use, the strategists will relay instructions back to the whips, who will then inform the delegates. The coordination will be so tight, said Mike Russell, the coalition's spokesman, "that there can be not just a message of the day, but a message of the hour or the minute" (Goldberg 1996a).

More important than technological wizardry, of course, was the fact that the vast majority of delegates to the convention held deeply conservative views largely in line with the positions of the Christian Coalition. A survey of GOP national convention delegates showed that the group overall was far more conservative than voters in general elections who identified themselves as Republicans, giving the edge to groups such as the Christian Coalition in pushing platform issues. The same survey found that 60 percent of the delegates opposed a platform plank that declared the GOP tolerant of different views on abortion; only 38 percent said that abortion should be allowed in cases of rape and incest; and 57 percent favored organized prayer in public schools (Bennet 1996b).

Influencing Party Platforms

Because candidates are not bound by them, many analysts are quick to dismiss party platforms as irrelevant. Indeed, 1996 GOP candidate Bob Dole announced that he had not read the platform and would not take the time to do so. Many interest groups, however, take a different view and have made strong efforts—particularly in recent years—to influence the platforms of both political parties. Interest groups assign symbolic importance to the creation of platforms that reflect their policy preferences, and they also believe that candidates do ultimately heed platforms to some degree. Moreover, interest groups are aware that because platforms receive considerable media coverage, they become important documents in the "battle of ideas."

Interest groups are probably correct in assigning importance to platforms. In the words of William Greener, the 1996 GOP convention manager, "I challenge or defy people to identify a better indicator of what a party will do during a campaign—much less what they will do in office—than the party platform." There is, moreover, empirical evidence that presidents do make an effort to fulfill many of the promises in their platforms. Political scientist Gerald Pomper reports that presidents have fulfilled approximately 75 percent of the specific pledges in their platforms, and the *Washington Times*—surely no friend to Bill Clinton—credited him with having fulfilled 47 percent of his campaign and platform promises during the first ten months of his presidency (Moss 1994; Pomper with Lederman 1980).

Party platforms are drafted by a platform committee, which may hold one or more hearings to allow interest groups to testify. Groups sometimes arrive with long lists of platform planks. In 1984, for example, labor unions, feminists, and other groups succeeded in inserting lengthy and detailed provisions into the Democratic platform, allowing Ronald Reagan to attack Democratic nominee Walter Mondale as a candidate of special interests. Subsequent Democratic platforms have been far less detailed and occasioned far less open conflict.

In 1992 and again in 1996, Clinton supporters dominated the Democratic Platform Committee. Because party rules allowed the nominee a great deal of ultimate control over the platform, issue activists had no opportunity to take over the convention proceedings and write the platform (Maisel 1996, 80–87). Although, for example, representatives from diverse groups in the party coalition made up the 1992 drafting committee, Democratic National Committee chair Ron Brown allowed the Clinton campaign to choose about one-half of the members of the committee (Maisel 1996, 81–82). The group most influential in drafting the platform language was Clinton's Democratic Leadership Council (DLC), an organization of moderate party leaders committed to moving the party toward the ideological center and away from the perception of being dominated by "special interests" on the left.

In 1996, the Democratic Platform Committee held a marathon one-day hearing in Cleveland at which representatives from the Sierra Club, Americans for Democratic Action, Veterans of Foreign Wars (VFW), the America-Israel Public Affairs Committee (AIPAC), and the American Petroleum Institute, among many others, testified (Maisel 1996, 82–83). Political scientist Sandy Maisel reports that some groups were more effective than others at both getting their viewpoint heard and influencing the convention. He notes that AIPAC was particularly effective: the group not only testified at the Cleveland hearing but also succeeded in getting strongly pro-Israel activists selected to both the drafting and platform committees. Ultimately, the wording of some sections of the platform document reflected AIPAC's influence (Maisel 1996, 84).

Union activists also played a major role in drafting the party platform, which included a section entitled "Standing Up for Working Americans." The platform staked out such pro-labor stances as pension protection, job training legislation, and a ban on replacing strikers. Yet overall, the platform was clearly controlled by Clinton supporters who wanted a moderate document from which to wage the presidential campaign.

In contrast, the GOP platform has in recent years provoked highly visible conflict between party moderates and anti-abortion Christian conservatives, and nominees have not always succeeded in controlling the language of the document. The chair of the RNC, in consultation with the party nominee, selects the chair and vice chairs of the platform committee, and each state delegation sends one man and one woman to the committee. Interest group members run for slots on the platform committee. Thus, in order to ensure the selection of platform committee members who hold particular views, interest groups vie to obtain a majority within the state delegation. In 1996, for example, Massachusetts governor William Weld worked hard, but unsuccessfully, to create a pro-choice majority among state delegates who would, in turn, send pro-choice delegates to the platform committee.

In 1992, former RNC chair Rich Bond selected a committee that traveled across the country, holding hearings and taking testimony from various groups on policy issues. The information gathered at these events was turned over to the convention platform committee to assist in deliberations on format and content. According to Bond, although President Bush wanted to retain control of the platform document and his campaign pressured the head of each state delegation to do everything possible to get sympathetic people selected to the platform committee, the platform was ultimately a highly conservative document that seemed ill-suited to Bush's moderate Republicanism. Maisel argues, however, that the Bush campaign appointed conservative chairs and vice chairs in an effort to appease inter-est groups and activists on the party's right wing (Maisel 1996).

In 1996, GOP nominee Bob Dole lost a highly publicized battle on lan-guage addressing the abortion issue. The platform committee adopted a strongly anti-abortion plank, and pro-choice advocates failed to get the full platform committee even to approve a supplemental official minority report in the document, even though they needed only 27 of 107 mem-ber votes (Republicans for Choice Report 1996). Although Dole was per-sonally anti-abortion, his campaign managers believed that it would be advantageous to have a "tolerance plank" stating that the GOP respected the right to hold different views on some controversial issues such as abor-tion. Dole tried to forge language for a tolerance plank that would be acceptable to both sides and made personal appeals to some of the interest group leaders and platform committee members, but as one conservative leader commented, "Dole thinks it's '68, when the candidate could pick up the phone and dictate the platform." The members of the platform com-mittee had been elected in their states with grassroots support from con-servative groups, and their agenda for the convention simply differed from that of the party's presidential nominee. Many of the delegates, at the urg-ing of leaders of conservative groups, had signed on with Dole merely because they knew that their chances of being elected to the convention and influencing the platform would be improved by siding with the like-ly winner (Drew 1997, 108).

When Dole quipped at the end of the convention that the platform was irrelevant to his campaign and that he had no intention of even reading the document, his statements appeared calculated to signal to more moderate voters that he did not plan to run on the hard-right positions of his own party's platform. Christian Coalition executive director Ralph Reed, how-ever, considered it a major victory that the anti-abortion plank in the party platform had been forged by grassroots activists elected as delegates rather than by the party nominee (Drew 1997, 109).

Financing Convention Activities

Although the two national conventions are partially financed by public funding, costs are increasingly likely to exceed the public grant. Each of the 1996 national conventions cost over $25 million, and over one-half of that funding came from the private sector.

Corporations donated large sums of money to help defray costs, sponsored events for the parties and their candidates, and, most important, contributed many of the goods and services that make conventions work. Many of the small and large corporations that provide funding for the conventions do so to retain the goodwill of party leaders, but there are sound business reasons as well. Approximately one-fifth of the 1996 GOP convention delegates were millionaires, and another one-fifth were worth at least $500,000—making the convention a good occasion for entrepreneurs to show off their wares.

At the 1992 party conventions, the first ones at which cellular phones were in widespread use, delegates' cellular phones were constantly busy and subject to eavesdropping. For the 1996 GOP convention, Ericsson Corporation, the pioneer in secure digital communications, donated three hundred of its phones (which also allow for paging, faxing, call waiting, and have a caller-identification feature) for delegates to use. Not only did the company make an impression on a lot of well-heeled Republican delegates, it also captured the attention of policy makers and the media. News reports of the advantages of the Ericsson technology brought the company more publicity than almost any paid advertising campaign could have (Goldberg 1996b).

In 1996, AT&T gave about $1.5 million to the GOP convention to help supply computers and cable wiring for on-line broadcasting. The company spokesman cited business incentives for the donation, which provided "the opportunity for us to showcase our technology and to help the Republican National Convention or the party put on a very expensive event" (Jackson 1996a). Subsequently, the GOP designated AT&T the official long-distance carrier at the convention. General Motors donated the official car, and United Airlines was the official airline. The chairman of the San Diego host committee, Gerald R. Parsky, claimed that politics had absolutely nothing to do with any of the corporate contributions: "Our sponsors' motivations for contributing to the host committee are nonpartisan in nature. . . . Their primary focus is a combination of a desire to contribute to the community and a desire to showcase their company in a commercial way" (Labaton 1996).

Much of the impetus for public funding of party conventions came from the ITT scandal of 1972. During the Nixon administration, the Justice Department investigated the ITT Corporation for antitrust violations. The Nixon campaign solicited a donation from ITT, and the corporation ultimately donated $400,000 to the Republican National Convention in Miami.

Although the Federal Election Campaign Act amendments of 1974 mandated public rather than private funding for conventions, the law allowed local businesses in host cities to provide special convention discounts. The Federal Election Commission (FEC) significantly softened this regulation in 1994, with a new interpretation that permitted local businesses to donate products to conventions for "promotional purposes" (Labaton 1996). Companies showered delegates to the 1996 conventions with free disposable cameras, Frisbees, and many other gifts with brand names advertised on the products. These "freebies" seemed benign enough and attracted little criticism, if any.

But Stephen Labaton of the *New York Times* reported that despite claims of nonpartisan, civically oriented motivations for giving, the largest donations to the two major party conventions in 1996 did, in fact, come from industries with substantial stakes in current legislation and federal regulations. The vice president of Anheuser-Busch, a large brewing company, admitted that although his company's donations to the two party conventions were in the spirit of promoting civic life, the corporation did plan to lobby delegates about the elimination of a 1991 federal tax increase on beer (Labaton 1996).

William Harris, manager of the 1992 GOP national convention, noted that local companies often provide important services for the conventions, in part to show the convention city in a good light to the rest of the country. Although the law does allow local businesses to donate money to host committees as a form of civic boosterism, it is worth noting that not one Fortune 500 company is headquartered in San Diego, the host city for the 1996 GOP convention. As long as a company could claim some local connection, however, it was allowed to make a contribution to the host committee. In the following exchange, a CNN reporter and William Grebe, chair of the GOP Convention Arrangements Committee, discuss contributions made to the host committee by Philip Morris, the tobacco company. The conversation illustrates just how tenuous the connections have become:

CNN: Philip Morris has a strong business connection to San Diego?

Grebe: Sure they do.

CNN: What's the connection?

Grebe: Kraft Foods. I assume people here buy Kraft Foods products. I know they think a lot of Miller beer. So sure, they have a connection here. And maybe some San Diegans actually smoke (Jackson 1996a).

Political parties use conventions to raise soft money contributions from corporate executives, generally offering access to party leaders at special events in exchange for contributions. At the 1996 GOP convention, the party offered each contributor donating $15,000 a chance to meet personally with House Speaker Newt Gingrich and to play in an exclusive golf tournament. For $25,000, donors could attend a horse race and reception at the Del Mar racetrack—events that, according to the *New York Times,* attracted twenty-five contributors of $25,000 and another fifty contributors of at least $100,000. One contributor of $250,000, the vice president of a large corporation, beamed that he and other contributors had been "surrounded by governors" and by "other GOP leaders" (Goldberg 1996b). The GOP gave contributors of at least $250,000 "season tickets"—invitations to all the major party events leading up to and during the convention, skybox seats at the convention, and the opportunity to have their photos taken with Dole and Kemp (Drew 1997, 117).

For the 1996 Democratic National Convention in Chicago, at least seventy-three companies contributed $100,000 or more to the host committee. United Airlines, one of the large contributors, was designated the official convention airline. Other corporate givers included Ameritech, Anheuser-Busch, Archer Daniels Midland, Chrysler, Lockheed Martin, Montgomery Ward, Motorola, Paine Webber, Quaker Oats, Sears & Roebuck, and Xerox. Among the most generous was Ameritech, a telephone company that spent in the millions to provide a telecommunications network for the media; free, prepaid phone cards and elaborate buffets for reporters; parties for delegates; entertainment for politicians and other leaders at its convention skybox; and an off-site trade show where participants could explore Ameritech technology and services (Wayne 1996).

Public interest organizations charged that the sharp increase in corporate contributions to the 1996 conventions violated the spirit of campaign finance regulations and included open attempts to buy access to policy makers. At the Chicago convention, Rep. Edward Markey, Mass., the ranking Democratic member of the telecommunications subcommittee that oversees companies such as Ameritech, praised the company's large contribution and said that through its efforts at the convention, "Ameritech has gained a tremendous marketing boost." Speaking at the company skybox, Markey added:

> You have assembled a fairly sizable percentage of opinion leaders here: you've got members of Congress, heads of many major corporations and

the most important reporters. They can spread the word when something
impresses them favorably. This is a chance for Chicago and for Ameritech
. . . to affect how they are viewed (Wayne 1996).

Conspicuous at both 1996 national conventions were the many lavish
events sponsored by lobbyists, trade associations, unions, and corporations.
Although congressional ethics rules prohibit a member of Congress from
accepting a dinner from a lobbyist, that same member is permitted to
accept a meal and even be honored at a widely attended event. This distinction is based on the assumption that a member accepting a private dinner or a gift from a lobbyist who has business before the government
would be indebted to the lobbyist, whereas at a widely attended event,
there is no one person to whom the member might potentially feel gratitude.

For both businesses and members of Congress, the benefits of a widely
attended event are substantial. Businesses do not have to report their
expenses to the FEC but may report the events as "business expenses" for
tax purposes. Members of Congress, even those who are designated as the
guests of honor, do not have to report these events as in-kind political contributions.

The 1996 national conventions were ideal occasions for well-attended
events sponsored by groups with an interest in government policy. At the
GOP convention in San Diego, Sen. Frank Murkowski, Alaska, chairman
of the Senate Energy and Natural Resources Committee, was feted by a
party sponsored by the natural gas industry, which also sponsored a party
to honor the chairman of the House Republican Conference, Rep. John
Boehner, Ohio. Rep. Jim Leach, Iowa, chairman of the Banking Committee, was honored by a reception sponsored by the securities industry. A dinner on a railway train sponsored by the Union Pacific rail company feted
Rep. Bud Shuster, Pa., chairman of the Transportation Committee. A leading tobacco lobby and the Mortgage Bankers Association jointly sponsored
a luncheon for Sen. Christopher Bond, Mo. The Minnesota-based Pills-
bury Company sponsored a salute to the Minnesota congressional delegation. Three representatives from Illinois were feted by the Chicago Mer-
cantile Exchange. Sen. John McCain, Ariz., chairman of the Commerce
Committee, was the honoree at an American Trucking Association luncheon. The U.S. Chamber of Commerce hosted a cruise in honor of the
GOP House freshmen, who were also honored at a reception cosponsored
by the Beer Institute, Philip Morris, and the law firm of Williams & Jensen.

The Food Marketing Institute sponsored breakfasts and dinners honoring various influential members of Congress (Drew 1997, 114–121; Master Calendar of Events 1996; Verhovek 1996).

Although the national conventions attract the most attention, many state parties hold conventions as well. In a few cases, candidates are actually selected or endorsed at conventions; more commonly, conventions provide an opportunity for the party to rally behind the nominee chosen through primary elections or caucuses. State conventions also perform other important functions: they adopt state party platforms, which sometimes differ significantly from those of the national party; they create and modify party rules for the distribution of resources and the selection of nominees; and they are often the forum for the selection of the state party chair, state committee members, and state representatives to the national party committee. In presidential election years, the state conventions sometimes make the final selection of delegates to the national conventions.

Generally, delegates to state conventions are chosen through a multistage process that includes local caucuses, congressional district conventions, and sometimes regional conventions. In most states, it is not especially difficult to become a state convention delegate, and in some states almost anyone who wants to attend can do so. Indeed, it is not uncommon for party leaders to "beat the bushes" to find enough delegates to represent their geographic area at the state convention.

Interest groups play an active role in state conventions. Table 2-2 shows the percentage of attendees at GOP conventions in five states who indicated that they were members of various interest groups. Few delegates were members of labor unions, environmental groups, feminist, or pro-choice groups. The percentage who were members of business and professional groups varied across the states: in Virginia, more than 50 percent of the delegates were members of professional groups, whereas in Florida, more than 60 percent of the delegates were members of business groups. The percentage who were members of pro-family, conservative Christian, and anti-abortion groups also ranged widely: more than half of Minnesota delegates were members of anti-abortion groups, versus less than one-third in Virginia. Nearly half the Florida delegates were members of pro–gun rights organizations (Green, Rozell, and Wilcox 1995).

At the huge (14,000-delegate) GOP nominating convention in Virginia in 1993, Christian right delegates threw the nomination for lieutenant governor to Michael Farris—former state chair of the Moral Majority and former attorney for Concerned Women for America—despite the fact that he had never held elected office. In 1994, at an equally large Virginia convention, Christian right and NRA delegates helped to nominate Oliver North, a former White House aide and participant in the Iran-contra affair, as a candidate for the U.S. Senate; North was perhaps the only Republican in the state who could not defeat incumbent Democratic senator Charles (Chuck) Robb (Rozell and Wilcox 1996).

In Oklahoma, in 1988, Christian right delegates who supported Pat Robertson succeeded in passing a party platform that included the following points:

- Teaching the "traditional cultural heritage of our country"
- Opposition to NEA involvement in the schools because the NEA "advocates sex education, ERA passage, abortion, sex clinics, nuclear freeze, a humanistic curriculum, and opposes traditional value systems"
- A requirement that students say the Pledge of Allegiance daily
- Opposition to "the current advocacy of Secular Humanism in any form in the public schools because it is a violation of the First Amendment"
- Opposition to the "utilization of mind-altering techniques" for public school students
- Opposition to state-mandated sex education in schools
- Opposition to school-based health clinics that dispense birth control and provide abortion counseling
- Insistence that AIDS education emphasize abstinence outside of marriage
- Opposition to the teaching of values education, death education, and situation ethics
- Opposition to the "New Age Movement philosophy, including reincarnation, mystical powers, Satan worship, etc., as introduced in the textbooks of our education system" (Hertzke 1993, 167–168).

The 1992 state GOP platform in Washington denounced the teaching of witchcraft and yoga in public schools (Appleton and Francis 1997). In

TABLE 2-2

Attendees at State Republican Party Conventions Who Identified
Themselves as Members of Interest Groups, 1993–1995

	Virginia	Washington	Florida	Minnesota	Texas
Business	36%	43%	61%	47%	39%
Professional	53	44	58	51	46
Labor	2	N.a.[a]	N.a.	N.a.	N.a.
Civic	41	37	73	54	46
Fraternal	17	15	27	19	15
Community	50	34	45	43	34
Education	23	26	37	28	26
Environmentalist	9	6	14	9	5
Pro-choice	7	4	5	5	6
Feminist	1	N.a.	N.a.	N.a.	N.a.
Women	N.a.	17	20	15	16
Church	N.a.	74	76	88	86
Conservative Christian	28	38	39	31	45
Pro-family	N.a.	37	28	42	43
Religious	63	37	25	53	40
Pro–gun rights	28	36	45	30	39
Anti-abortion	30	44	38	53	50
Taxpayer	N.a.	15	23	15	12
Conservative	N.a.	48	48	47	48

Source: Survey data collected by the authors and by John C. Green.

Note: Entries are the percentages of all attendees at state party conventions who indicated membership in each type of group. Each respondent could claim membership in multiple groups.

[a] Not asked.

Virginia, 1994 party resolutions called for a constitutional amendment to ban all abortions, denounced the state's sex education program as encouraging students to engage in "sexual immorality," and included a statement that the GOP was proud of the state's "Colonial, Confederate, and American heritage," and that "to ensure that military firearms suitable for militia be readily available to the twentieth-century militia of Virginia, . . . semiautomatic rifles are twentieth-century militia firearms" (Rozell and Wilcox 1996).

Democratic state platforms have in recent years also adopted controversial positions on issues such as affirmative action, parental notification on abortion, and welfare reform. In the 1960s and 1970s, state Democratic political parties were often deeply divided over civil rights issues. In 1964, for example, Mississippi sent two different delegations to the Democratic National Convention, which chose to seat the civil rights delegation.

State conventions often select state party chairs and committee members as well. Because the policy preferences of party officeholders can have profound effects on party policy, interest groups offer encouragement, support, and training to help their members and supporters secure election to party office.

In Texas alone, for example, the Christian Coalition held at least twenty-five training sessions for members planning to run for the important position of party precinct chair. Precinct chairs select the delegates to state senatorial-district party conventions; at those conventions, chairs for the state senatorial districts are chosen, and delegates are selected for the state convention. The Christian Coalition fielded candidates for 80 percent of precinct chair positions, winning many of them (Bruce 1997). In 1994, nearly two-thirds of state party convention delegates were conservative Christians, more than half of whom had never attended a party meeting before. These activists drove the sitting party chair from office, and the convention defeated several referenda that would have officially proclaimed that the party included members with a range of views (Bruce 1997).

In recent years, efforts on the part of the Christian right to influence—and even control—state Republican Party committees have been highly successful. In 1994, *Campaigns and Elections,* a Washington, D.C., political magazine, reported that the Christian right was the dominant force in GOP politics in nineteen states and had substantial influence in another twelve. Reacting to this news, Christian Coalition founder Pat Robertson told a coalition gathering in 1995, "I'm glad to see all this they say about thirty-one, but that leaves . . . a lot more. We've got more work to do. Because I like 100 percent, not 60 or 70" (Edsall 1995). In many states, Christian right activists control a substantial number of precinct, county, and other party committees, enabling group members to channel party resources for the benefit of candidates that they support, to schedule official meetings to discuss policy, and to adopt party rules that make it easier for Christian right candidates to win nomination.

Although the Christian right is the most visible and active set of interest groups in internal, state-level party politics, labor unions, civil rights groups, farmers' groups, and others have been active in Democratic politics; and in some states, members of one or another of these groups are the dominant faction in the Democratic Party. Nevertheless, the efforts of the Christian right to control the GOP are unique in American history and may indicate a profound change in the relationship between social movement organizations and political parties.

SUMMARY

Changes in party rules over time have created an opportunity structure that allows interest groups to be active players in intraparty politics. Involvement in political parties is attractive to groups with broad policy goals, especially social movement organizations that seek to transform social relationships or "moral policy."

Specific tactics include recruiting interest group members and sympathizers as candidates, training candidates to run in party primaries, and providing endorsements, financial support, and volunteer labor to assist candidates in their quest for nomination. Interest groups also work to send delegates to state and national party conventions and to change the language of party platforms to include explicit endorsement of their policy goals.

Finally, interest groups sometimes seek to change the personnel not only of government but also of the party itself. They may encourage their activists to become members of party committees or even to run for the position of local or state party chair. Obtaining such positions sometimes enables interest group activists to rewrite party rules in ways that are favorable to candidates who share their policy preferences and to direct party resources toward the goals of their particular group.

Groups with more narrow goals also participate in party politics, but in very different ways. Corporations have become major sponsors of conventions, hosting lavish parties and receptions for party leaders. Such groups are often neutral in intraparty contests but show general support for the party as part of an access strategy, seeking to cultivate ongoing relationships with party leaders to further their lobbying goals.

Once parties select their nominees and approve their platforms, candidates move on to the general election. American elections are costly affairs, and candidates must raise hundreds of thousands of dollars for House races and millions of dollars for senatorial and presidential contests. Interest groups work closely with candidates as well as with parties, communicating their views and their support. The next chapter will explore the relationship between parties and candidates.

CHAPTER 3

Interest Groups and Candidates

On any evening during an election campaign, the nation is alive with fund-raising activities, and interest groups are likely to be involved in virtually every one. At a political action committee (PAC) fund raiser in Washington, D.C., PAC officials present their checks, shake the hand of the host—an incumbent member of the House—have a drink, eat a bite, and swap political gossip. In her home state, an incumbent senator holds a fund-raising dinner, arranged with the help of an interest group, at which several tables were "purchased" by other groups. At campaign headquarters, a presidential candidate telephones corporate executives, asking for contributions to the party or the campaign. At a direct-mail fund-raising firm, staff members are preparing solicitations to send to a list of interest group members the firm has rented for a candidate; in the solicitations, the candidate makes a special pitch on issues of concern to the group's leaders.

As noted in Chapter 1, one of the organizing principles for our exploration of interest groups and American political life is the communication between interest groups and the individuals or entities they hope to influence. Although such communication is often complex and directed at multiple audiences, the focus in this chapter is on interest groups and candidates: What do groups want to "say" to candidates, and how do they get their message across?

Put simply, financial or in-kind contributions facilitate much of the communication between interest groups and candidates. Interest groups donate money directly to candidates; channel money through PACs, contribute "soft money" to parties; and provide a wealth of goods and services for candidates, parties, and campaigns.

We begin the chapter by looking at the strategic context: how is communication between interest groups and candidates shaped by laws, regulations, and common practice on the one hand and by the groups' goals and resources on the other? Next, we examine one of the primary vehicles for both raising and channeling the financial contributions of interest groups and their members: the political action committee. The chapter looks in detail at the history and resources of PACs, as well as at how they determine their contribution strategies. We then examine the various ways in which interest groups manage to "give beyond the limit"—to make contributions that exceed what regulations allow. Next, the chapter explores interest groups' contributions to political parties—including "soft money" donations, which play an increasingly important role in financing elections. Finally, we discuss contributions of goods and services, an uncommon but effective way for interest groups to gain greater control of the use of their money and to maximize the impact of their contributions.

THE STRATEGIC CONTEXT: REGULATIONS, GOALS, AND RESOURCES

In this section of the chapter, we first consider how funds from interest groups make their way into the electoral process. Like the state regulations and party rules that shape interest groups' involvement in party politics, campaign finance laws—and judicial interpretations of them—create an opportunity structure within which interest groups must work. Given that opportunity structure, interest groups select various strategies and tactics, which will in turn be shaped by the goals the groups are pursuing and the resources they have available.

The Evolution of Campaign Finance Regulation

Interest groups have made direct cash contributions to candidates throughout American history. In the latter part of the nineteenth century, corporations helped finance national elections—and also bribed some members of Congress and the executive branch. Mark Hanna, an industrialist who raised funds for Republican William McKinley's 1896 presidential campaign, approached many major corporations and suggested donations based on the firm's revenues, warning that the administration would not do business with companies that failed to contribute. The excesses of the McKinley fund-raising efforts made the role of interest groups in financing elections more visible than ever before, and in 1907, the Tilman Act banned banks and corporations from making contributions to federal candidates. By the 1930s, organized labor had become involved in campaign finance: through Labor's Non-Partisan League, unions gave more than $1 million to federal campaigns (Wright 1996). During World War II, direct contributions from union treasuries were banned by passage of the Smith-Connally Act, in 1943—a change made permanent by passage of the Taft-Hartley Act in 1947.

Although corporations and unions could not draw political contributions from their treasury funds, they found ways to be active in politics. Corporations often gave their executives "bonuses," then directed them to pass the extra money along to specific candidates. Labor chose another route: in 1943, the Congress of Industrial Organizations (CIO) formed a PAC that collected voluntary contributions from union members and contributed it to candidates. Because the PAC was not technically a labor union and the contributions were voluntary (although union treasury funds did pay the operating expenses of the PAC), unions believed that their PAC was not subject to the ban on union contributions. In 1955, the American Federation of Labor and the CIO merged, and the combined AFL-CIO created COPE, the Committee on Political Education, which quickly became the most important political arm of organized labor (Gerber forthcoming). By the 1960s, other unions had formed PACs, as had professional associations such as the American Medical Association (AMA). Business groups were represented by the Business-Industry Political Action Committee (BIPAC), which encouraged corporate involvement in elections. But in the 1960s, unions were by far the best represented in the PAC universe.

Although the legality of PACs was questioned almost from the beginning, the Supreme Court did not rule on the issue. In 1968, however, a federal trial court and a court of appeals ruled that labor PACs violated the Taft-Hartley Act and sentenced officials from a labor union to fines and jail terms. Many labor activists feared that the Supreme Court would uphold the convictions and order the dismantling of COPE. In 1971, as Congress was drafting the Federal Election Campaign Act (FECA), unions pressured their congressional allies to include language that would legalize PACs. An amendment drafted by AFL-CIO lobbyists and introduced by Rep. Orval Hansen, R-Idaho, allowed both corporations and labor unions to form

PACs. Labor strategists believed that the benefit of retaining COPE outweighed the potential danger that corporations would form PACs; indeed, by the early 1970s, few had done so (Epstein 1980). However, urged on by BIPAC, corporations mobilized quickly to form PACs.

In the 1972 presidential campaign, despite the fact that corporate contributions were illegal, Richard Nixon's Committee to Reelect the President chose to follow the McKinley model, recommending contribution targets for corporations—a tactic that worked especially well when the company had business before the White House. The campaign solicited a contribution from the ITT Corporation at a time when the company badly wanted antitrust relief, and the committee received donations from milk producers before the president raised supports on milk prices. The campaign laundered many corporate gifts through Grand Cayman Island, and the campaign official in charge of corporate contributions eventually went to jail (Sorauf 1988).

Information uncovered during investigations of Nixon's reelection campaign led Congress, in response to public and media pressure, to create an entirely new regulatory regime. In 1974, Congress amended the language of the FECA. The amendments established a campaign finance system with four main elements: limits on contributions, limits on spending, public funding, and disclosure.

LIMITS ON CONTRIBUTIONS. The law permitted private individuals to give $1,000 to each candidate for national office for each election in which that candidate was involved. Because most candidates run in primary as well as general elections, individuals can ordinarily give $2,000 to any candidate.[1] Interest groups were permitted to form PACs that could collect voluntary donations of up to $5,000 per year from each of their members and contribute up to $5,000 to candidates in any federal election.

The law limited the amounts that party committees could give to candidates or spend on their behalf. Individual contributions to all kinds of political committees—parties, PACs, and candidates—were limited to $25,000 per year. There were also limits on the amounts that candidates could contribute to their own campaigns. Contribution limits were not indexed to inflation, and the 1974 values remain in force today.

LIMITS ON SPENDING. The amendments limited spending by candidates for Congress and the presidency and also limited what individuals and PACs could spend independently to urge the election or defeat of candidates. Moreover, the law held that independent expenditures could not be made in coordination with campaign officials.

PUBLIC FUNDING. The amendments provided public funding for presidential elections, but provisions for funding congressional elections were dropped from the final bill. The law established a public fund created by checkoffs on federal income tax returns; today, taxpayers can designate $3 of their taxes to be diverted to that fund. The Federal Election Commission (FEC) uses this money to provide matching funds for presidential candidates during primary campaigns, to help pay for the major party conventions, and to provide a public grant for major candidates during the general election. During the primary election and caucuses, the fund is used to match the first $250 given by any individual to qualified presidential primary candidates. Under this system, a donation of $1,000 to Bob Dole in 1996 would thus have been worth $1,250 to the campaign because the federal government matched only the first $250, whereas a contribution of $25 to Pat Buchanan was worth $50 because the entire amount was matched. During the general election, public grants in equal amounts are given to the nominees of the two major parties, and under some circumstances to candidates of minor parties.[2] In 1996, the Clinton and Dole campaigns received roughly $61 million each from the government to finance their campaigns, and Ross Perot received approximately $29 million.

DISCLOSURE. The amendments established a single agency, the Federal Election Commission, to enforce the law and to collect and disseminate information about the financing of national elections. The commission creates rules and brings action against violators, but there are six commissioners—three Democrats and three Republicans—and it takes four votes to make policy. As a consequence, the FEC is not an aggressive regulatory agency, but it does play an important role as the repository of campaign finance data. All candidates, PACs, and party committees that participate in federal elections are required to file regular reports with the FEC, which then makes this information available to the public in a variety of formats.[3]

The 1974 FECA amendments did not limit the ability of interest groups to communicate with their members about elections or to endorse candidates. Nor did the amendments regulate "nonpartisan" voter mobilization efforts undertaken by nonprofit groups; such efforts are under the regulatory eye of the IRS, which has the power to deny tax-exempt status to organizations whose activities are not genuinely nonpartisan. The new regulations did, however, impose a comprehensive framework on campaign financing—which was almost immediately altered by the Supreme Court.

Legal challenges to the FECA amendments were undertaken by an unusual coalition of liberal and conservative groups and activists, including the American Conservative Union and the New York chapter of the American Civil Liberties Union. The plaintiffs alleged that the law violated freedom of speech by limiting the amounts that individuals and groups could contribute and spend independently to advocate their ideas.

In January 1976, in *Buckley v. Valeo,* the Court ruled that campaign spending is protected by the First Amendment because it involves political speech, but that Congress can regulate contributions in the interest of preventing corruption or the appearance of corruption. This ruling struck a delicate and tenuous balance between protection of free speech and prevention of corruption. It left intact all requirements that candidates, PACs, and party committees disclose the sources and use of their funds. The court also upheld limits on contributions from individuals, PACs, and party committees, as well as limits on spending by parties on behalf of candidates, holding that these limits helped government prevent corruption and the appearance of corruption.

However, *Buckley* eliminated all limits on spending by candidates and all limits on independent expenditures by individuals and PACs, holding that such limits would constitute an abridgment of free speech. The Court upheld the public financing of presidential elections and ruled that candidates who accepted public financing could be bound to spending limits in exchange for the public grant. In essence, the Court ruled that contributions could be limited because they might lead to corruption or the appearance of corruption, whereas spending could not be limited because it is protected free speech.

The distinction between contributing and spending seems arbitrary, and the logic does not withstand close inspection: for example, a PAC associated with a large group such as the National Rifle Association (NRA) or the AMA can devote millions of dollars in independent expenditures to help elect a candidate but can give only $10,000 to that candidate for primary and general election campaigns. The rationale of the distinction is that a larger gift—of perhaps $50,000—might corrupt the candidate but that a huge independent expenditure would not. It seems likely, however, that an incumbent who has benefited from a massive independent spending campaign will be as grateful to the interests that financed that campaign as he or she would be to a group that gave the money directly to the campaign. Similarly, if the First Amendment protects the right of a group of citizens to spend unlimited amounts of money to argue that Sen. Barbara Boxer, D-Calif., deserves a second term in the U.S. Senate, why would it not also protect that group's right to give the money directly to Boxer so that she can make the case herself?

Although the distinction between spending and contributing may be arbitrary, the Court was attempting to balance two critical values that appeared to be in conflict. Political speech is clearly at the heart of the First Amendment, and election campaigns constitute a clear and central form of political speech. On the other hand, the government clearly has a compelling interest in preventing corruption. Although it is easy to imagine other distinctions the Court might have drawn, any attempt to balance these two principles would perhaps be arbitrary.

In 1979, Congress passed additional amendments to the FECA that allowed individuals and interest groups to give gifts of unlimited size to political parties for "party building" and to help elect state and local candidates. When interest groups make these "soft money" contributions, they are not required to use money collected through PACs but can instead use treasury funds that come from business profits or membership dues. Technically soft money may not be spent to advocate the election of specific candidates or given to candidates for federal office. However, parties may use soft money for a variety of other purposes—for salaries and office facilities, for voter mobilization, to help local or state-level candidates, and to run advertisements for the party, for example.

In 1996, the Supreme Court allowed interest groups to spend money on "issue advocacy" campaigns as long as they did not expressly advocate the election or defeat of a particular candidate. Like funds for soft money contributions, funds for issue advocacy can be drawn from interest groups' treasuries. Thus, an interest group can spend unlimited sums from its treasury on television advertisements criticizing an incumbent member of Congress—as long as the ads avoid a list of specified words and phrases such as "vote for" and "select." Although the advertisements themselves may be indistinguishable from those funded by independent expenditures, they differ in two important respects: they can be paid for with treasury funds, and the spending need not be disclosed to the FEC.

Goals and Resources

We suggested in Chapter 2 that most intraparty electoral activity is undertaken by interest groups pursuing electoral strategies, which are designed to change the personnel of government. Campaign contributions are made by interest groups pursuing electoral strategies, access strategies, or both: contributions to candidates in close elections can help influence who wins, and using contributions to maintain friendly relations with powerful incumbents—often committee chairmen and party leaders—can help lobbyists gain access to policy makers. Because committee chairs and party leaders rarely face opposition in party primaries and are unlikely to be involved in close elections, there is little incentive for interest groups pursuing an access strategy to seek involvement in intraparty politics or to mount issue advocacy campaigns. For interest groups pursuing an access strategy, contributions to campaigns and political parties are thus most likely to be the primary form of electoral involvement.

Of course, interest group involvement in campaign financing requires money. For an interest group to make direct contributions to candidates, its members must not only be sufficiently motivated to give to their PAC and to candidates that the group endorses but must also have the financial resources to do so. Having a large membership is helpful because individual contributions to PACs and to specific candidates are limited. Because soft money contributions come directly from interest group treasuries, an interest group's overall financial well-being is also a factor.

Tactics for channeling money into campaigns vary widely. Interest groups can form PACs, raise money from their members through voluntary contributions, and give this money directly to candidates—but there are limits on the amount that a PAC can give to any particular candidate. PACs can purchase or produce goods and services for a campaign and give them to the candidate as an in-kind contribution, although such contributions are subject to the normal limits. Members of interest groups can also give to the candidate as individuals, and lobbyists or PAC directors can collect those gifts into a bundle and pass them along to the candidate; although each member is limited in the amount he or she can contribute, there is no limit to the amount that a group can collect. Interest group members and their families can purchase seats at tables at fund-raising dinners; the group is credited with the large donation, although each donation is assessed against individual limits.

Interest groups can use their treasury funds as well, donating soft money in unlimited amounts to party committees. Although by law, soft money must be used for party building or to assist state or local candidates, in practice, much of this money ends up aiding candidates for national elections.

PACS: AN OVERVIEW

After the passage of the FECA amendments in 1974, the Sun Oil Company formed a PAC and asked the FEC to comment on its legality. In 1975, the FEC issued the SUNPAC advisory opinion, which approved of the corporate PAC and allowed Sun Oil to pay indirect and overhead costs from the corporate treasury. Once the FEC gave the green light to the business community, the late 1970s and early 1980s saw an explosion in the number of corporate PACs. The apparent success of ideological PACs (such as the National Conservative Political Action Committee) in the 1980 presidential election spawned a surge in the formation of other ideological PACs in the early 1980s. By the mid-1980s, more than 4,000 PACs were registered with the FEC. Since then, the number of PACs has remained relatively constant, with just over 4,500 registered during the 1996 election cycle and 4,079 remaining at the end of 1996. (See Table 3-1.)

The sheer number of PACs is misleading, however, because fewer than two-thirds of the committees on the FEC books in 1996 were active in financing elections:only 2,900 PACs both raised funds and contributed money to the 1996 elections.[4] PACs that have ceased campaign activity linger on the roster for several reasons: they may simply have neglected to file the paperwork to terminate the PAC; they may owe money to vendors; or they may hope to become involved in campaign finance again soon. The FEC periodically removes the names of inactive PACs from its database, but it allows them to remain for a time because the PACs may become active again.

Most PACs are segregated funds of interest groups; that is, they are discrete accounts containing money raised according to FECA regulations and kept separate from the operating funds of the sponsoring organization. A PAC need not have a separate office or even a full-time director—merely a separate bank account. PACs vary widely in their size and organization: some are large bureaucratic bodies with full-time staff, offices, and equipment, whereas others are administered by an interest group official whose primary duties lie elsewhere and who can devote only a few hours per week to the PAC.

Corporations sponsored more than half the active PACs in 1996; when trade association PACs are included, the proportion of PACs representing corporate America swells to approximately two-thirds. In contrast, labor represents only 8 percent (233) of all active PACs. Although PACs sponsored by professional associations or membership groups made up a very

TABLE 3-1

Number of PACs by Type and Election Cycle, 1978–1996

Election cycle	Corporate	Labor	Trade, membership	Nonconnected	Total[a]
1978	785	217	453	162	1,653
1980	1,206	297	576	374	2,551
1982	1,469	380	649	723	3,371
1984	1,682	394	698	1,053	4,009
1986	1,744	384	745	1,077	4,157
1988	1,816	354	786	1,115	4,268
1990	1,795	346	774	1,062	4,172
1992	1,735	347	770	1,145	4,195
1994	1,660	333	792	980	3,954
1996	1,642	332	826	953	4,079

Source: Compiled from Federal Election Commission data.

Note: Numbers are as of December 31 in election year.

[a] Includes PACs associated with cooperatives and corporations without capital stock, not shown separately.

small portion of the total, committees sponsored by groups such as the National Association of Realtors (NAR), the AMA, and the NRA were among the largest and most innovative committees (Bedlington 1994, forthcoming; Gusmano forthcoming).

Not all PACs are sponsored by a preexisting interest group: any individual or group of individuals may form a PAC, collect voluntary contributions from citizens, and make contributions to candidates. Nearly one-fifth of active PACs in 1996 were "nonconnected" (that is, had no sponsoring or parent organization), and perhaps two-thirds of these were either quasi-party groups seeking to assist Republican or Democratic candidates or ideological groups seeking to elect candidates with specific views.

Figure 3-1 shows the percentage of active PACs in 1996 associated with corporations and trade associations, labor unions, professional groups and membership organizations, and ideological causes. (Percentages for trade associations and professional and membership organizations are estimates. Because the laws that regulate their behavior are the same, FEC records combine these three types of committees.) As the figure demonstrates, corporations and trade associations dominate the world of PACs. Corporate executives argue, however, that their numerical advantage is misleading

FIGURE 3-1
Active PACs by Type

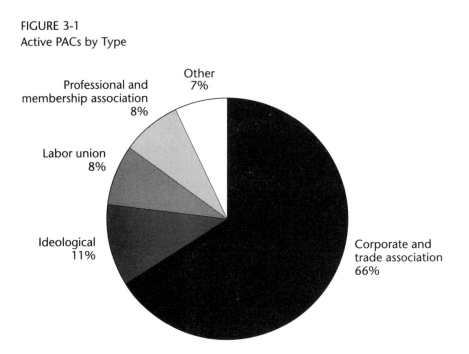

Source: FEC data provided by Robert Biersack, who also assisted with the construction of the estimates.

because labor PACs are larger on average than corporate committees and give more money to candidates. There is some truth to this claim: in the 1996 elections, corporate and trade association PACs outnumbered labor committees by eight to one, but their net advantage in direct contributions to candidates was closer to two-and-a-half to one.[5] Moreover, as we will see in the next chapter, labor involvement in campaigns reaches far beyond campaign contributions. Table 3-2 shows the advantage that corporate and labor union PACs have in campaign contributions. Moreover, most of the soft money contributions described later in this chapter are from business: in 1996, corporate PACs outspent labor PACs by nine to one.[6]

Who Forms PACs and Why

Interest groups can participate in elections without forming PACs. Most of the activities described in Chapter 2—recruiting and training candidates, sending delegates to party conventions, working to influence party

TABLE 3-2

PAC Contributions to Candidates for Federal Office by Type and Election Cycle, 1978–1996 (in millions of dollars)

Election cycle	Corporate	Labor	Trade, membership	Nonconnected	Total[a]
1978	$9.8	$10.3	$11.3	$2.8	$35.2
1980	19.2	13.2	15.9	4.9	55.2
1982	27.5	20.3	21.9	10.7	83.6
1984	35.5	24.8	26.7	14.5	105.3
1986	49.4	31.0	34.4	19.4	139.4
1988	56.1	35.5	41.2	20.3	159.2
1990	58.1	34.7	44.8	15.1	159.1
1992	68.4	41.4	53.9	18.3	188.9
1994	69.6	41.9	52.9	18.2	189.6
1996	78.2	48.0	69.1	24.0	217.9

Source: Compiled from Federal Election Commission data.

[a] Includes PACs associated with cooperatives and corporations without capital stock, not shown separately.

platforms—can be undertaken without a PAC. Interest groups can select candidates to endorse and communicate those endorsements without ever forming a PAC. Interest group members can attend fund-raising dinners for candidates and parties without forming a PAC. Interest groups can even spend unlimited amounts from their treasuries to promote policy positions (and, indirectly, candidates) and can contribute unlimited amounts—also from their treasuries—to party committees, all without forming a PAC. An interest group must form a PAC, however, if its leaders want to gather contributions from members, aggregate those contributions, and—as official representatives of the interest group—give candidates money.

Although many PACs are active in American elections, a majority of corporations, trade associations, and membership organizations do not have PACs. PACs are more common among labor unions, but a number of unions have not formed PACs or have terminated PACs that were once active. Large companies, trade associations, and membership groups are more likely to form PACs than their smaller counterparts—in part because larger organizations are able to raise more PAC revenue and are therefore better able to play the PAC game and in part because large firms, associations, and membership groups are more likely to be affected by legislation and regulations.

Among corporations, PACs are most common in regulated industries, in industries where companies frequently interact with government, and in industries that compete for government contracts. In many organizations, the decision to form a PAC begins with an organizational entrepreneur who promotes the idea and takes responsibility for running the PAC (Ferrara 1994). PAC formation also appears to be contagious: when a few PACs have formed in a given industry, other companies may follow suit, perhaps because corporate officials believe that they must keep pace with their competitors. Indeed, political scientist Larry Sabato quotes one PAC official from the U.S. Chamber of Commerce who suggested "only slightly facetiously" that some corporations formed PACs because the CEO found himself surrounded on the golf course by CEOs from companies with PACs (Sabato 1984, 31).

For many interest groups, forming a PAC makes little sense. To begin with, PACs are expensive: overhead costs to the parent organization run between 50 and 100 percent of total PAC revenues (Sorauf 1984). To raise money, PAC officials may have to make awkward solicitations of colleagues. And incumbents constantly ask PAC officials for campaign contributions, creating potentially awkward refusals. Most important, however, many PACs raise so little money that they can make only a handful of contributions, which may be of little benefit to lobbyists. Fully one-third of PACs active in the 1996 election cycle gave to six or fewer candidates, and 10 percent of active PACs gave to a single candidate. Most small PACs probably accomplish very little for their parent organizations.

Yet forming a PAC does have certain advantages. In some organizations, the PAC serves as the focus for the organization's involvement in elections. For members, it provides an alternative, easy form of political participation; for the parent group, it provides more frequent opportunities to communicate with members. And for those organizations that can raise enough money, the PAC may help influence a close election or help lobbyists maintain good relations with an important committee chair.

PAC Resources

A number of factors determine the resources available to PACs: regulations affecting fund raising; the PAC's relation to its parent organization; and the size and complexity of the PAC organization itself.

The money that PACs contribute to candidates or spend independent-ly must be raised in voluntary contributions from the members of the organization, and each member is limited to a contribution of no more than $5,000. The regulations are quite specific about who can be solicit-ed by various types of organizations: corporations may solicit executive and administrative personnel and their families and stockholders and their families at any time; regular employees may be solicited twice a year. Labor unions may solicit members and their families at any time, and twice yearly they may solicit nonmember employees of a company where union members are employed. Membership organizations may solicit their members and executive and administrative personnel and their fam-ilies at any time.

Nonconnected PACs are not sponsored by organizations with members and are thus allowed to solicit the general public. Most do so by mailing solicitations to individuals who might be sympathetic to their issue agen-da. Potential contributors are usually identified through "prospecting": PACs rent membership lists from sympathetic organizations or subscrip-tion lists from publications that have special appeal to individuals who might contribute, then mail solicitations to the list. Rental agreements usually allow the PAC to use the list only once, but anyone who responds to the initial mailing can be placed on the PAC's own mailing lists and resolicited.[7]

Being able to solicit the general public may appear to give nonconnect-ed PACs an advantage, but the advantage in fact lies with PACs sponsored by interest groups. Interest groups that sponsor PACs can pay overhead costs (for example, salaries, supplies, postage) from their treasuries and can therefore channel all the money they raise into contributions to candidates and expenditures on their behalf. Because nonconnected PACs must pay all their costs out of the contributions they receive, much of the money raised goes not to candidates but to overhead expenses. Overall, less than 30 percent of the funds raised by nonconnected PACs is channeled to con-tributions or independent expenditures; the rest pays for running the PAC. Some ideological PACs run up large debts to the direct-mail companies who solicit contributions for them, and the life span of such organizations is often short. Only 40 percent of nonconnected PACs registered with the FEC in 1996 were active in the 1996 election cycle, and many of the oth-ers had outstanding debts.[8]

Sponsored PACs vary in the resources they receive from parent organi-zations. Some organizations pay for several full-time employees, for example, while others pay for a single part-time staff position. AT&T PAC, sponsored by the telecommunications giant, has an executive committee, separate committees to handle fund raising and contributions at the national level, and state and regional committees—a structure that allows the PAC to carefully gather and evaluate information about each race.

The AFL-CIO's COPE can draw on the expertise of local, regional, and state committees as well as on the capacities of the local, state, and national unions that are members of the AFL-CIO (Gerber forthcoming; Wilcox 1994). COPE has a professional staff that gathers and disseminates information to other committees; COPE briefings are attended not only by other labor unions but also by a number of other PACs in the Democratic coalition.

PACs with large staffs can gather information about the elections—the closeness of the race, the positions of the nonincumbent, the level of commitment to a candidate from party committees or other interest groups. A PAC with a single part-time employee, in contrast, operates with much less information. Taken together, such disparities in resources greatly affect the ability of a PAC to be active in national campaigns.

Among each type of PAC—corporate, trade, labor, professional, ideological—there are a few large and sophisticated committees, a larger number of medium-sized committees, and a large number of small PACs with few resources. Interest groups with large and dedicated memberships are able to raise substantial sums of money. In the 1996 election cycle, EMILY's List, a PAC that helps fund the campaigns of pro-choice Democratic women candidates, raised more than $12 million in member contributions, for example, and the NRA's PAC raised more than $7 million. Other PACs are associated with organizations with fewer and less supportive members and therefore had far less money to contribute to candidates.

Although PACs contributed more than $215 million to federal candidates during the 1996 election cycle, most of this money was given by a few very large PACs, and most PACs gave smaller amounts. More than 55 percent of all contributions in the 1996 election cycle were given by the largest 180 committees, and a quarter of all PAC contributions were made by just thirty-three PACs, each of which gave more than $1 million. In contrast, the 2,200 smallest PACs combined gave less than 13 percent of all PAC contributions (FEC data).

In 1996, AT&T PAC, historically the largest corporate PAC, contributed more than $1 million to House candidates and more than $200,000 to Senate candidates (Mutch 1994, forthcoming). In contrast, the PHH Corporation, a small private company in the transportation industry with only one part-time employee assigned to its PAC, raised less than $8,000 during the 1996 election cycle and gave nearly that amount to seven House and Senate candidates (Rossotti 1994).

In the 1996 election cycle, COPE gave approximately $1 million to House candidates and another $200,000 to Senate candidates, almost all of whom were Democrats. In addition, COPE gave more than $350,000 to party committees, and the AFL-CIO gave $500,000 in soft money contributions to national Democratic Party committees and additional contributions to state and local party committees. In contrast, the Buffalo Local 222 Aluminum Brick and Glass Workers PAC made two contributions to federal candidates totaling $400 (FEC data).

Among ideological PACs, the National Right to Life Committee gave more than $146,000 to candidates for federal office in 1996; it also made independent expenditures, distributed information and cash to state anti-abortion PACs, and engaged in voter mobilization drives. The South Dakota Pro-Life PAC, in contrast, gave $900 to three candidates. (FEC data) Although both of these committees were anti-abortion PACs, their organizational characteristics and capacities had little in common.

Table 3-3 shows the concentration of PAC contributions in 1990 and 1996. In both election cycles, most PACs gave small amounts to federal candidates. Half of all active PACs in 1996 gave less than $15,000, and three-quarters gave less than $55,000. Clearly, the largest and smallest PACs face very different decisions about how much to give and to whom. The data in this table make clear that those who are concerned that PACs may have disproportionate influence in American politics should concentrate on the few very large committees that dominate the PAC world.

PAC CONTRIBUTION STRATEGIES

PACs routinely receive more invitations to fund-raising events than they can ever afford to attend, and they are solicited by more candidates than they can ever afford to support. In determining how best to use their resources, PACs generally make two kinds of decisions: first, what types of candidates to support; second, which specific candidates to support.

Although many PACs lack any explicit statement of policy on what types of candidates to support, PACs making contributions to congressional candidates generally pursue a mixture of access and electoral strate-

TABLE 3-3
Concentration of PAC Contributions, 1990 and 1996

	Percentage of total contributions	Number of committees[a]	Percentage of committees[b]
1990 contribution range			
$0	0	1,640	35
$1–$5000	1	1,207	26
$5,001–$50,000	14	1,224	26
$50,001–$100,000	11	255	5
$100,001–$250,000	22	227	5
$250,001–$500,000	15	69	1
$500,001–$1,000,000	15	34	1
Over $1,000,000	21	21	0
1996 contribution range			
$0	0	1,517	34
$1–$5000	1	910	20
$5,001–$50,000	12	1,307	29
$50,001–$100,000	11	353	8
$100,001–$250,000	19	261	6
$250,001–$500,000	15	93	2
$500,001–$1,000,000	17	54	1
Over $1,000,000	26	33	0

Source: Compiled from Federal Election Commission data.

[a] The number of committees whose contributions fell within each range.

[b] The percentage of the total number of active committees represented by Number of Committees.

gies. PACs pursuing an access or legislative strategy give money as part of their lobbying effort, to gain the ear of incumbents who can influence legislation of interest to the parent organization. This usually means giving to party leaders, committee and subcommittee chairmen, and other important actors in the policy network who can influence the content of a bill and its chances of passage, regardless of their ideology or whether they are involved in a close election. In the 1996 election cycle, more than four hundred PACs gave only to incumbents. The Greater Washington, D.C. Board of Trade Federal PAC, for example, gave nearly $100,000 to incumbents of both parties but did not contribute to a single nonincumbent candidate. A large majority of these incumbent-oriented PACs, which constituted approximately 14 percent of all active committees, were small to mid-size corporate and trade association committees.

Incumbents who hold powerful positions in Congress are generally able to solicit contributions from access-oriented PACs. The campaign staff of an influential incumbent may call a PAC director and ask for a contribution or offer an invitation to a campaign fund-raiser—an offer that the PAC director may feel reluctant to refuse. PACs whose sponsoring organizations hope to have continued access to party leaders or committee chairs give money to ensure that they are seen as friends of those in power. It is no accident that party leaders in the House routinely receive far more PAC money than do other members: House Speaker Newt Gingrich, R-Ga., received more than $1 million in PAC contributions in the 1996 election cycle, and PACs also gave to other organizations with which Gingrich was associated (such as GOPAC, discussed in a later section of this chapter). Important committee chairs also receive disproportionate amounts of PAC money: in 1996, Sen. John Warner, R-Va., chairman of the Senate Defense Committee, led all candidates, with nearly $1.5 million in PAC receipts—including more than $200,000 from PACs representing defense companies and more than $70,000 from executives and others employed by those companies (www.crp.org).

An electoral strategy, in contrast, aims to ensure that Congress has the largest possible number of members who favor the policy positions of the interest group. Nonconnected and ideological PACs generally pursue electoral strategies, as do labor committees.

PACs that follow an electoral strategy often give substantial amounts of money to nonincumbent candidates who share their views. In 1996, approximately one in four active committees gave at least half their money to nonincumbents. Handgun Control Voter Education Fund, for example, gave more than $200,000 to congressional candidates in 1996, and more than 60 percent of that money went to challengers and candidates for open seats.

Since their goal is to elect as many sympathetic members of Congress as possible, PACs pursuing an electoral strategy give not only to nonincumbents, but also to incumbents in close races who share the parent group's policy goals. As the fortunes of the parties ebb and flow, electorally oriented PACs redirect their contributions from incumbents to challengers, targeting contributions where the money might influence the outcome of the election. If, for example, a PAC prefers policies that are more likely to be supported by liberal Democrats, then that PAC will support endangered Democratic incumbents in electoral cycles where Republicans are likely to gain seats, as in 1994; when Democrats are expected to gain seats, the same PACs will support Democratic challengers and candidates for open seats, as in 1996. Electorally oriented PACs that prefer the policies of conservative Republicans would follow the opposite course. The practice of supporting incumbents or challengers, depending on the prevailing electoral winds, is often called "strategic contributing."[9]

The way that contributions are solicited makes it difficult for PACs to give solely to incumbents or nonincumbents. Party leaders routinely ask PACs to give to the most promising nonincumbent candidates, and committee chairmen often echo the request, leading even the most access-oriented PACs to contribute to at least a few nonincumbent candidates in order to keep important policy makers happy. At the same time, many electorally oriented PACs find it difficult to refuse solicitations from powerful incumbents who have a strong record of supporting a particular ideological position. Such "friendly" incumbents may repeatedly ask an ideological PAC for a gift, and if polling data suggest that the incumbent may indeed face a close election, it is difficult for an ideological PAC to refuse.

Indeed, PAC directors often complain that when the most powerful members of Congress ask them to give, they have no choice but to comply. Former senator Lloyd Bentsen, D-Texas, the 1988 Democratic vice presidential candidate and chairman of the Senate Finance Committee, had a program of special breakfasts that could be attended by PAC directors who contributed $10,000 to his campaign. When the chairman of the committee that writes the tax laws affecting your industry invites you to eat eggs and grits and talk taxes, it is hard to refuse. Party leaders also pressure PACs to give, and their staff scrutinize the contribution records of PACs to identify those that give "too much" to the other party.

Data on the patterns of PAC contributions will help us get a closer look at which types of candidates receive PAC support. Table 3-4 shows both the amount and proportion of money that PACs contributed to different types of candidates. In 1980, 63 percent of PAC contributions went to incumbents; in 1992, 73 percent; and 1996, 67 percent—indicating that most PAC contributions are given as part of lobbying efforts and reflect access strategies. Indeed, many of these contributions went to incumbents who faced no real prospect of defeat: in 1996, a majority of PAC contributions went to incumbents who were assured of victory. For example,

TABLE 3-4
PAC Contributions to Major Party Federal Candidates: 1980, 1992, and 1996

Type of candidate	1980		1992		1996	
	Contribution	Percentage of total contributions	Contribution	Percentage of total contributions	Contribution	Percentage of total contributions
House Democrats						
Incumbent	$16,934,165	29	$67,106,187	36	$51,712,687	24
Challenger	2,342,807	4	7,866,490	4	16,737,142	8
Open seat	2,071,601	4	13,407,388	7	10,932,119	5
House Republicans						
Incumbent	$9,054,494	16	$31,978,807	17	$65,698,926	30
Challenger	5,784,253	10	4,564,352	2	4,856,130	2
Open seat	3,004,611	5	7,394,537	4	9,135,646	4
Senate Democrats						
Incumbent	$7,459,436	13	$20,027,952	11	$7,511,408	4
Challenger	1,011,366	2	6,455,164	3	2,843,745	1
Open seat	816,199	1	5,695,317	3	9,061,322	4
Senate Republicans						
Incumbent	$2,862,646	5	$16,598,062	9	$21,213,241	10
Challenger	5,690,944	10	3,176,774	2	4,570,582	2
Open seat	1,319,888	2	4,272,660	2	10,273,264	5
All incumbents	36,310,741	63	135,711,008	73	146,136,262	68
All challengers	14,829,370	26	22,062,780	11	29,007,599	13
All open seats	7,212,299	12	30,769,902	16	39,402,351	18
Total	$58,352,410		$188,543,690		$214,546,212	

Source: Compiled from Federal Election Commission data.
Note: Columns may not add up to 100 percent because of rounding.

corporate PACs directed 52 percent of their contributions to candidates for the House who faced little electoral challenge, while 36 percent went to those who faced strong opposition (Herrnson 1997).

Contributions to nonincumbents are usually channeled to candidates for open seats, although this pattern may not be evident from the data in this table. Because challengers significantly outnumber candidates for open seats, especially in the House of Representatives, even when all challengers receive slightly more money than all candidates for open seats, open-seat candidates receive far more PAC money per candidate than do challengers. In the 1996 House races, candidates for open seats averaged nearly $165,000 in PAC money, whereas challengers averaged just over $50,000. In contrast, incumbents averaged nearly $300,000 in total PAC receipts.

The data in Table 3-4 show other trends as well. First, in 1980, many PACs (mostly corporations and other pro-Republican organizations) gave substantial support to GOP challengers, a trend that persisted throughout most of the 1982 election cycle. Republican Party officials enticed corporate contributions by holding out the promise that the GOP might capture the House in 1982. After the Democrats gained twenty-six House seats in 1982, however, most corporate PACs—under pressure from Democratic Party leaders—abandoned Republican challengers. In 1980, Republican challengers in the House and Senate received 20 percent of all PAC contributions, but by 1992 that figure was down to 4 percent.

Second, a comparison of the percentages for 1992 and 1996 shows that many access-oriented PACs switched their contributions to Republicans when that party took control of Congress in 1994. Republican incumbents received 26 percent of all PAC contributions in 1992 and 40 percent in 1996, while Democratic incumbents' share of PAC contributions fell from 47 to 27 percent. Of course, there were more Republican incumbents and fewer Democratic incumbents after the 1994 elections, but on average, the GOP received far more PAC money when it had control of the congressional agenda. The average House Republican incumbent received slightly over $200,000 in PAC money in 1992 and nearly $300,000 in 1996.

Many PACs switched their patterns of party giving after 1994. In 1992, the General Electric PAC contributions favored Democrats by a margin of three to two, but in 1996, Republicans were favored by a margin of almost two to one. The Federal Express PAC gave 62 percent of its donations to

Democrats in 1992 and 70 percent to Republicans in 1996. AMPAC, the American Medical Association's PAC, gave 51 percent of its contributions to the GOP in 1992—a percentage that increased to 81 in 1996. Finally, RJR Nabisco's PAC strongly favored Democrats in 1992 but gave 73 percent of its contributions to Republicans in 1996 (Shields 1997). Overall, corporate, trade, and nonconnected PACs substantially increased their contributions to GOP candidates. (See Table 3-5.)

The switch to GOP incumbents has been accelerated by pressure from Republican policy makers and party leaders. After the 1996 elections, Republican National Committee (RNC) chair Haley Barbour blasted the Business Roundtable—a group representing two hundred chief executive officers of large corporations—for having been insufficiently loyal to the party:

> The fact remains that much of the big-business community—led by its
> flagship organization the Business Roundtable—chose to remain bipartisan
> and did nothing differently in the face of this onslaught by the united
> Left—led by the Washington labor bosses (BIPAC 1996).

After taking over Congress, the GOP began pressuring pro-business groups to drop their bipartisan strategies and to increase contributions to Republican candidates (Stone 1997).

Influences on Strategy Selection

How do PACs decide what mix of access and electoral strategies to pursue? The most important factors are the policy agenda of the sponsoring organization; the type of sponsoring organization (for example, corporate, labor, or ideological); and the level of available resources.

POLICY AGENDA. Some interest groups seek narrow, particularistic policies that will benefit only their organization. Corporations and trade associations, which may seek a specific exemption from regulation or a narrowly targeted tax break, are particularly likely to pursue particularistic policies. Other groups pursue broader policy goals: labor unions, for example, support policies that stimulate employment and offer protection against the hardships of economic downturns; and business groups such as the National Federation of Independent Businesses (NFIB) support policies that will keep interest rates and labor costs low and reduce government regulation in general.

TABLE 3-5
Changes in PAC Allocation by Type: 1992, 1994, and 1996

Type of candidate	1992		1994		1996	
	Contribution	Percentage of total contributions	Contribution	Percentage of total contributions	Contribution	Percentage of total contributions
Corporate						
Republicans	$31,976,016	50	$32,872,432	51	$52,057,218	73
Democrats	32,308,294	50	31,430,922	49	19,096,942	27
Labor						
Republicans	1,914,644	5	1,598,642	4	3,023,413	7
Democrats	37,577,358	95	38,987,257	96	43,379,845	93
Trade, membership, and health						
Republicans	21,436,982	42	23,249,504	46	36,539,188	65
Democrats	29,899,090	58	27,015,672	54	19,758,192	35
Nonconnected						
Republicans	6,472,913	37	7,012,460	40	13,413,910	60
Democrats	11,010,957	63	10,471,935	60	8,947,346	40

Source: Compiled from Federal Election Commission data.

Interest groups that seek narrow benefits may find that they can be obtained from incumbents of either party; the PACs of these groups may therefore contribute funds to the campaigns of powerful committee chairmen and leaders of the majority party. If a few or even one committee in the House or Senate is able to distribute the benefits an interest group seeks, its PAC may focus contributions on members of those committees. PACs that seek particular benefits from government seldom give to challengers or to candidates for open seats because such candidates are unlikely to be in a position to deliver special policy benefits in the near future.

Interest groups that seek broad economic policies such as cuts in business taxes or protection for striking workers are more likely to support candidates of a single party and to try to increase that party's strength in Congress. Interest groups with broad economic-policy goals pursue electoral strategies, targeting PAC aid to races where it will do the most good. Labor union officials generally believe that broad policies that help unionized workers are more likely to win support when the Democrats control government and thus seek to maximize the number of Democratic seats in Congress. The NFIB is closely linked to the Republican Party for similar reasons (Shaiko and Wallace forthcoming). Yet BIPAC has occasionally supported Democratic candidates, arguing that its goal is merely to create a "business-friendly" Congress, not merely a Republican one (Nelson 1994; Nelson and Biersack forthcoming).

Ideological groups that hold particular views on controversial issues such as abortion and gay rights sometimes create strong links with a single party; Christian Coalition officials, for example, attend Republican conventions and often behave as if the coalition were an adjunct to the party. Some ideological groups, however, support candidates of both parties when it is in their interest to do so: the National Abortion and Reproductive Rights Action League (NARAL) contributes mostly to Democratic candidates but also supports pro-choice Republicans (Thomas forthcoming).

Like other interest groups, ideological organizations use a mix of access and electoral strategies, and groups with the same objectives sometimes pursue competing strategies. For example, the NRA favors GOP candidates most of the time but occasionally backs Democrats who favor gun rights. The more extreme Gun Owners of America (GOA) is less likely to consider a bipartisan strategy. In 1997, the two groups were at odds over endorsements in a state legislative race in Virginia, where the NRA backed the pro–gun rights incumbent Democrat over an even more conservative Republican challenger backed by the GOA. The NRA candidate won by just several hundred votes, giving the Democrats a bare legislative majority in the chamber.[10]

The disagreement in this case mirrors a larger debate among leaders of ideological PACS. The NRA decision to back a pro–gun rights Democratic incumbent reflects the organization's desire to retain lobbying access to Democratic legislators. If the NRA tried to persuade Democratic lawmakers to support their bills—but always backed Republican candidates, no matter how strongly the opposing Democrats hewed to the NRA line—their lobbyists would soon find the doors of many Democrats closed. The GOA's decision to back an even stronger pro-gun Republican reflects the view that the best way to protect gun owners' rights and roll back gun control is to create a legislature that has a strong GOP majority composed of members who favor gun rights.

RELATIONSHIP WITH THE SPONSORING ORGANIZATION. Corporations and trade associations have generally pursued access-oriented strategies, directing more than 80 percent of their total contributions to incumbents of both parties. Business groups generally prefer Republicans to Democrats, but they readily gave to Democratic incumbents when that party controlled Congress. When they did give to nonincumbents, however, they showed their partisan preference; in 1992, more than two-thirds of all contributions that corporate PACs made to nonincumbent candidates went to Republicans. Until 1994, partisan preferences and an interest in supporting incumbents pulled corporate PACs in opposite directions, but GOP control of Congress has eliminated most of this conflict and created a strong tendency to support Republican incumbents.

Labor unions have long and deep ties to the Democratic Party and in most election cycles give 90 percent of their money to Democratic candidates. Many labor PACs practice strategic contributing, giving money to protect incumbent Democrats in years in which Republican gains are expected and shifting to nonincumbent Democrats in years in which gains are expected for that party. Figure 3-2 shows the percentage of all labor PAC contributions going to incumbents from 1982 through 1996. Note, for example, that in 1982, in the midst of a deep recession when many nonincumbent Democrats defeated Republican officeholders, labor committees gave almost half their contributions to nonincumbents. In 1984, when the economy was in recovery and President Ronald Reagan's popularity raised the possibility that Republicans would ride into Congress on his coattails, labor committees gave a substantial majority of their funds to

FIGURE 3-2

Percentage of Labor PAC Contributions Going to Incumbents, 1982–1996

Percentage

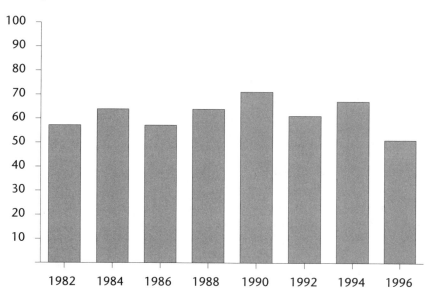

Source: Compiled from Federal Election Commission data.

vulnerable Democratic incumbents. Similarly, in 1994, as the GOP surge captured control of the House and Senate, labor PACs directed most of their contributions to vulnerable incumbents, whereas in 1996, when the Democrats hoped to regain control of the House, these PACs gave nearly half their contributions to nonincumbents.

Although most labor PACs pursue electoral strategies, corporate committees show significant diversity. Some consistently throw their resources behind GOP challengers for the House and Senate, despite the risk of irritating powerful Democratic committee chairmen. In some cases, these PACs are influenced by an entrepreneur—perhaps the firm's founder, perhaps someone within the organization who pushed to form the PAC. The Eaton Corporation's Public Policy Association, for example, was formed in 1977 by former Eaton chairman John Hushen, who had served as deputy press secretary to President Gerald Ford. Hushen chaired the PAC and directed its contributions to Republicans, including many challengers and candidates for open seats. After the 1992 elections, an internal corporate reconsideration of the PAC's strategy led to its dissolution (Ferrara 1994). In contrast, corporate PACs that allow lobbyists to take part in strategic decision making tend to support incumbents (Handler and Mulkern 1982). Indeed, those corporate PACs located in the Washington, D.C., area give significantly more money to incumbents than do those located outside the beltway (Eismeier and Pollock 1984; Wilcox 1989). Moreover, corporate PACs in regulated industries are more likely to support incumbents (Handler and Mulkern 1982).

AVAILABLE RESOURCES. Sometimes the precise mix of access and electoral strategies is a function of the PAC's overall level of resources. Consider, first, the more than nine hundred PACs that gave $5,000 or less during the 1996 election cycle, most of which made a small number of small contributions to candidates. Smaller PACs generally have little discretion in their contribution decisions. They generally give to the chairs and perhaps other members of committees with jurisdiction over their issues and to incumbents from districts where they have facilities; there is little or no money left for other contributions. Small labor PACs give to Democrats on key committees and to Democrats from the districts in which the largest concentrations of their members live. Small ideological PACs may give to one or more incumbents who show particular support for important policies.

Larger committees, however, can give to the most important incumbents in their legislative area—party leaders, powerful committee personnel, incumbents who represent important geographic areas (such as districts with company plants), and their strongest legislative allies—and still have money left over to "invest" in nonincumbent candidates (Eismeier and Pollock 1984; Wilcox 1989). In some cases, they may give to open-seat candidates who have proven friendly in state legislatures, or they may even give to challengers who appear to share their policy preferences. Sometimes this "venture capital" may go to a nonincumbent who is supported by a powerful incumbent patron or to a challenger to an antagonistic incumbent.

Influences on PAC Decision Making

Few committees have the resources to give in every race. Labor PACs are solicited by nearly every Democratic hopeful (including some who are running against each other in a party primaries), and access-oriented corporate committees are often solicited by nearly every incumbent member of Congress. Whatever mix of access and electoral strategies a PAC ultimately chooses, it must make decisions about whom to support and must develop rules about how to make those decisions. Party leaders, committee chairs, and important policy advocates, for example, are more likely to be supported, a strategy that is sometimes officially articulated in PAC contribution guidelines (Bedlington forthcoming). Some PACs give almost exclusively to party leaders and to members of a few crucial committees because these legislators are in a position to help the group achieve its policy goals.

Contribution decisions are shaped primarily by two factors: first, the structures and processes that operate within the PAC and within the sponsoring organization; second, the amount and type of information on candidates that the PAC is able to obtain.

Although PACs vary widely in how they make their contribution decisions, most have one thing in common: they are not democratic institutions. PACs generally do not solicit advice from contributors, and donors are usually technically powerless to influence PAC decisions. Nevertheless, donors who are unhappy with a PAC's contribution decisions can "vote with their feet" and simply refuse to contribute to the PAC in the future. Although few individual donors can exert much leverage with the threat of this sanction, few PACs can tolerate a significant decline in member giving. At least some PACs will therefore make small contributions to the favorite candidates of blocs of contributors, especially when these donors are local activists (Sorauf 1988). Few contributors make a big effort to influence PAC contributions, however; instead, most appear to treat PAC contributions as investments in a political "mutual fund" that diversifies their contributions among important policy makers and oversees the management of their political interests (Eismeier and Pollock 1985).

INTERNAL STRUCTURES AND PROCESSES. Smaller PACs may grant their director or an official of the sponsoring interest group complete discretion over contributions: the American Association of Publishers' PAC was run by one woman who was both PAC director and lobbyist and had a virtually free hand to direct contributions to whichever candidates she chose (Stronks 1994). Small nonconnected committees often allow their founders complete control over the allocation of funds: Morris Amitay, of the Washington PAC (a pro-Israel committee), runs the entire operation (Levick-Segnatelli 1994). Small corporate committees may be influenced by the founder of the company, who often pressures for a more electoral-oriented strategy, or the lobbyists, who generally push for a more access-oriented approach.

Larger PACs generally have formal rules that include explicit criteria for contributions; they may also have boards of directors whose members advise the PAC director and sometimes make final decisions about contributions. The board may be composed of individuals from all sectors of a conglomerate corporation, of individuals from state or local chapters of a union or other federated organization, or of individuals who have made large donations to a nonconnected PAC. Sometimes several committees participate in decision making. The NAR, for example, used to rely on one committee to determine contributions and another to determine independent expenditures: the committee that directed contributions had substantial representation from state and local Realtors, whereas the committee that directed independent expenditures reflected the strategies of the NAR national leadership (Bedlington 1994). Although large institutionalized PACs often develop bureaucratic approaches to decisions, they have proven willing to change their decision-making approaches (Bedlington 1994, forthcoming; Gerber forthcoming; Mutch 1994, forthcoming; Wilcox 1994).

PACs whose sponsoring organizations have strong state and local chapters often rely on suggestions from those chapters; local chapters of labor unions recommend candidates, as do local chapters of the Sierra Club (Cantor forthcoming). Although national PAC officials can and sometimes do override the recommendations of local units, they show restraint in doing so; alienating local activists may deprive the organization of the ability to rally volunteers for voter mobilization and other efforts. The NAR has gone so far as to create programs that allow local organizations to make small contributions without the approval of the national office (Bedlington forthcoming). Through their In-State Reception Program, instituted in 1994, local NAR officials may attend in-district fund-raising events and contribute up to $1,000 to an incumbent without the approval of the national board. Similar guidelines apply to fund-raising events for nonincumbents.

INFORMATION ACCESS. PACs with electoral strategies value information on just how close a given race is likely to be so that they can target their money where it will have the greatest impact. Some PAC officials commission polls; others read poll results on the World Wide Web. Some attend Washington briefings given by the AFL-CIO, BIPAC, or party committees; others subscribe to special publications that provide detailed looks at various elections across the country. Many PACs require evidence—such as polling data or fund-raising prowess—of the viability of nonincumbent candidates. Some PACs are associated with federated interest groups that have state and local chapters, and these PACs are often able to tap the expertise of local political actors for information on the electoral viability of candidates.

Many PACs consider the legislative record of incumbents. The NAR, for example, refuses to give to incumbents who have not supported its policies on crucial issues, and the Sierra Club will not contribute to candidates with poor environmental records. More recently, even AT&T PAC—which had traditionally given to most incumbents to ensure access—has begun to consider incumbents' voting records in its contribution decisions.

Although it is relatively simple to determine the voting records of incumbent members of Congress, PACs that give to nonincumbents face a more difficult task. In some cases, local units or activists may provide information about a nonincumbent candidate's record in a local council or state legislature. Some ideological PACs mail surveys to candidates and use the responses to help determine whom to support. Some PACs serve as information conduits, providing cues to PACs in a particular community. COPE, BIPAC, and other groups provide information on candidates' views and their prospects for election. When BIPAC tells corporations that it supports a candidate, it essentially guarantees the candidate's pro-business credentials. A BIPAC endorsement helps candidates raise money from corporate PACs because smaller committees that lack the ability to gather their own information often rely on such cues (Nelson and Biersack forthcoming).

GIVING BEYOND THE LIMIT

Any single PAC can give only $5,000 to any national candidate in any single election. The effective limit is therefore usually $10,000, because all candidates are presumed to run in primary elections even if unopposed. (The occasional runoff elections allow PACs to give as much as $15,000 to a single candidate.) In fact, few PACs make contributions of this size; a typical PAC in 1992 gave seven contributions averaging less than $1,000 each to House candidates and two contributions averaging less than $1,300 to Senate candidates (Wright 1996). But some PAC officials want to exceed the legal limits.

PACs seek to provide additional assistance to candidates for a variety of reasons. Electorally oriented PACs may identify a few close races that take on special symbolic significance (the election or defeat, for example, of an ideologically extreme candidate such as Sen. Jesse Helms, R-N.C.), or they may identify a few very close races that might tip the balance of the Senate or House or increase the number of members who share their policy views. Access-oriented PACs may want to establish a particularly cozy relationship with party leaders, committee chairmen, or other important policy makers. To do so, they may want to give beyond the limit—or the incumbent may ask them to.

How can PACs channel more money to a candidate than the legal limits allow? One method, discussed in the next chapter, is through independent expenditures—money spent on behalf of a candidate in an effort to obtain voters' support. But contributions that exceed legal limits can also be channeled directly to candidates—principally through practices called bundling and coordinating contributing and through donations to affiliated organizations.

Bundling and Coordinated Contributing

The total limit on PAC contributions does not apply to members of a PAC, each of whom can give up to $1,000 to a candidate in a given election or $2,000 for the entire election cycle; family members of PAC members can also make individual contributions. Because the PAC and its individual members and their families can give money, this creates the possibility for a single interest group to contribute a much larger amount of money to one candidate than one might otherwise suppose.

Moreover, the law allows PACs to bundle contributions from members; that is, the PAC can collect contributions that are either made out to the candidate or earmarked to the candidate through the PAC, then distribute those contributions to the candidate. Thus, the director of a corporate PAC might give $10,000 to an incumbent (the total permitted on behalf of the PAC) but also present an additional $30,000 in individual contributions from the corporation's executives and their families.

Bundling has become a controversial form of interest group electoral involvement, primarily because of the highly visible and successful efforts of EMILY's List, which bundled millions of dollars to pro-choice Democratic women candidates in recent election cycles. In 1996, EMILY's List claimed to have contributed—through direct contributions and bundling—$6.5 million to candidates it supported. This figure is impossible to verify, however, because the FEC does not require PACs to disclose bundled contributions of less than $200 (EMILY's List encourages their members to make contributions of at least $100). EMILY's List has become the model for other ideological PACs—including WISH List (Women in the Senate and House) and the Gay and Lesbian Victory Fund—that want to channel individual contributions to candidates (Rimmerman 1994, Rozell forthcoming).

Bundling is not the only way that interest groups can channel money from their members into the campaign coffers of candidates. PACs and interest groups can coordinate the giving of their members, even when they do not assemble their funds into a bundle. One such method is to sponsor tables at fund-raising events for candidates, a practice that is especially common in presidential and senatorial campaigns. This approach can be implemented through a PAC or by an organization without a PAC. Major events often have tables sponsored by several major companies and interest groups.

Coordinated giving also occurs when campaigns recruit fund raisers from within an organization, who then ask their colleagues for contributions. For example, when Michael Dukakis ran for president in 1988, the Dukakis for President campaign recruited the principal owner and chairman of Fidelity Investments, who successfully solicited fifty additional corporate executives and their spouses (Brown, Powell, and Wilcox 1995). The presidential campaigns of most mainstream candidates are financed by networks of contributors, many of whom are linked to interest groups. George Bush's 1988 campaign, for example, raised more than $35,000 from forty-nine members of a single Los Angeles law firm that represented defense contractors—far more than any PAC sponsored by the firm would have been allowed to give (Babcock and Morin 1988).

Each of these techniques allows interest groups—in some cases through their PACs and in some cases without them—to channel far more money to candidates than the FECA would allow through direct PAC contributions. Indeed, interest groups sometimes use these techniques instead of direct PAC contributions, for some candidates refuse to accept PAC donations. For example, Sen. David Boren, D-Okla., consistently returned any unsolicited PAC contributions, but the individuals who gave to his campaigns included many oil company executives, wildcatters, and their families. Collectively, coordinated giving from the oil industry provided Boren with significant resources, although none of it came through PACs.

Some interest groups sponsor fund-raising events and invite their own members. This tactic is especially popular with federated organizations because the candidate attends the event and therefore has multiple opportunities to interact with group members. In some cases, such events are sponsored jointly by several interest groups, or the sponsoring interest group may invite representatives from or members of another group to the event.

Finally, interest groups can rent out their mailing lists to candidates, enabling candidates to solicit group members directly for contributions. If the solicitation includes a personal endorsement by an interest group leader or activist, the mailing can raise significant sums for the candidate. In Virginia, the Family Foundation (a conservative pro-family group) rents its list to candidates, and the solicitation often includes a personal endorsement from the group's founder and former leader, Walter Barbee. According to Barbee, such mailings usually yield many individual contributions from group members.

It is important to understand, however, that not all contributions from company executives are coordinated through company or PAC officials. In fact, there has been little research on the level of coordinated giving by corporations, but ongoing research by one of the authors of this volume suggests that at least some of the time, the candidates supported by corporate executives may differ from those backed by the company PAC. Interest groups do bundle contributions and coordinate the giving of their members, but not all giving by interest group members is bundled or coordinated.

Giving to Affiliated Organizations

Thus far we have focused on direct contributions to candidates' principal campaign committees, but some powerful incumbents have other affiliated organizations as well. Many have formed or head their own national PACs, which raise money from individuals and other PACs and give that money to candidates. These "leadership PACs" serve a variety of functions: they can help a candidate launch a presidential bid by paying for travel costs and consultants (Corrado 1992); help a candidate in a bid for party leadership or the chairmanship of a committee; or help a candidate build legislative coalitions (Wilcox 1990).

For example, House majority whip Tom DeLay, Texas, heads Americans for a Republican Majority, a leadership PAC that in 1996 raised over $100,000 from other PACs, along with additional funds from lobbyists and other interest group representatives. Some PACs gave DeLay's campaign committee the maximum contribution of $10,000 for the primary and general elections, then contributed to DeLay's PAC as well. Not all PACs that gave to DeLay's PAC did so to avoid contribution limits; indeed, most had not given the maximum to his campaign committee. A few even gave to DeLay's PAC instead of to his campaign committee, presumably because DeLay did not face serious competition in 1996 and thus solicited contributions to his PAC to make it easier to centralize the distribution of this money to other candidates.

House minority leader Richard Gephardt's Effective Government Committee helps solidify his position as party leader in the House and is also part of his efforts to seek the White House. Many corporate, labor, and ideological PACs have contributed to Gephardt's PAC. DeLay's and Gephardt's PACs both attract contributions from committees with electoral as well as access goals. Some PACs give to these leadership PACs because they can channel the money into those campaigns that need it most, thereby influencing the composition of Congress. Yet many others give simply as an additional way of ensuring lobbyists access to influential party leaders.

House Speaker Gingrich's leadership PAC, GOPAC, works to increase Republican representation in elected bodies at all levels of government by recruiting and training conservative GOP candidates to run effective campaigns. GOPAC draws significant contributions from groups and individuals who are primarily concerned with the policy direction and electoral fortunes of the Republican Party. GOPAC conducts candidate training seminars throughout the country and often shares its training audiotapes and booklets with other conservative interest groups that recruit and train members and sympathizers to run for office (www.gopac.com).

In anticipation of a likely presidential run in 2000, former Tennessee governor and former Department of Education secretary Lamar Alexander has formed two PACs: a federal PAC that is subject to the $5,000 federal contribution limit and a Tennessee PAC that is not. Through the state-affiliated PAC, Alexander can raise unlimited amounts to engage in activities that will promote his presidential aspirations (Marcus 1997c). State PACs are governed by state law, and some states have contribution limits, but many do not. A surprising number of incumbent members of Congress have state PACs, which can be used to build political support for a member of the House or Senate, stave off a primary election challenge from someone within the party, or solidify a fund-raising base for a run for higher office.

In addition to PACs, some candidates sponsor foundations that can collect contributions from PACs and even from interest group treasuries. Although these foundations are not supposed to engage in explicitly political activity, some skirt the law, helping candidates from one party or those who share an ideological view or helping a candidate launch a presidential bid. Some foundations wish to influence the ideological direction of a party, others to spread democracy abroad, still others to raise and distribute charitable contributions. In each case, however, when an interest group contributes to the foundation, the candidate is aware of the donation, and the interest group generally hopes that the contribution will help its lobbying efforts.

In preparation for a likely presidential bid in 2000, publisher Steve Forbes has established an issue advocacy group called Americans for Hope, Growth, and Opportunity. Although it is not officially a campaign organization, Forbes is using the group to build a donor list and to enhance his standing with important interest groups in the GOP. By late 1997, Forbes had raised over $3 million through the group and built a donor network of over 75,000 individuals. In his 1996 presidential run, Forbes had difficulty attracting support from social conservatives because of his moderate stand on abortion. Aware of social conservatives' power in GOP nomination politics, Forbes is using his not-for-profit group to build goodwill with former opponents by making donations to groups such as the Christian Coalition's Catholic Alliance and Pat Robertson's Washington-based School of Government (Marcus 1997c). In many cases, foundations pay a candidate's travel expenses as he or she crosses the country building a political organization and may provide a mechanism for keeping consultants on retainer or even maintaining full-time staff.

Sen. Jesse Helms has been associated with a complex web of national and local PACs, foundations, and other organizations. In 1996, it was disclosed that the Jesse Helms Center had accepted $750,000 from R. J. Reynolds Tobacco Co. and $200,000 from Philip Morris Co., among many other large corporate contributions. Some, but not all, of the elements of the Helms empire have aided his reelection efforts; others simply promote his policy preferences. But large contributions to these groups are yet another way for interest groups to gain access to Helms.

CONTRIBUTIONS TO PARTIES

In addition to contributing directly to candidates, PACs and interest groups can donate to party committees. Unlike the activities described in Chapter 2, contributions to parties are generally not meant to influence the ideological positions of the parties but to gain access to party leaders or to help the party's candidates win election. In 1996, 41 percent of active corporate PACs gave to at least one party committee, as did a third of active committees associated with trade associations and membership groups, half of active PACs associated with labor unions, and less than a third of non-connected PACs. Some of the largest PACs gave to several national and state party committees. AT&T PAC, for example, made a number of contributions to party committees in the 1996 elections. (See Table 3-6.)

Although PACs can give to party committees, these gifts are limited by law to $15,000 to any one party committee in any one year. Interest groups, however, can contribute much more in the form of soft money, and these contributions need not come from PAC receipts; as long as the parties keep the funds in a separate account for specific activities, they can receive unlimited contributions directly from interest group treasuries. Soft money can be spent on "party building" or to help state and local candidates.

Although soft money cannot, in theory, be spent to help specific candidates for national office, in practice soft money contributions are often raised by or for candidates for federal office. Since 1984, presidential candidates have raised tens of millions of dollars in soft money for their parties and have generally been allowed to direct the spending of these funds. President Bill Clinton's fiftieth birthday party, at Radio City Music Hall, was merely one of many major soft money fund-raising events sponsored by Republicans or Democrats in 1996. In the 1996 election cycle, the two parties raised more than $263 million in soft money, far outstripping previous totals (www.fec.gov). The parties used this money to launch major media campaigns—campaigns that included ads that were, in many cases, virtually indistinguishable from those paid for by party hard money accounts.

Both parties have created special programs for major contributors of soft money. In 1996, the Democratic National Committee (DNC) offered individuals membership in the "Executive Committee" for a contribution of $100,000, promising an opportunity to meet with party officials and offer insight to policy makers. In exchange for an initial contribution of $100,000, an additional contribution of the same amount four years later, and annual gifts of $25,000 in the interim, the GOP offered membership in "Team 100." Congressional investigations in 1997 focused on Democratic soft money contributions from Asian governments and firms, which the party was forced to return; on calls made by Vice President Al Gore from inside his official residence; and on DNC fund-raising events that offered major donors the opportunity to have coffee with the president. In the 1996 campaign, President Clinton apparently allowed major donors (including some corporate executives) to sleep in the Lincoln bedroom of the White House—a practice that led to accusations that the president had

TABLE 3-6

AT&T PAC Contributions to Party Committees, 1996

	Number of gifts	Total
Federal Money		
Democrats		
Atlanta '88 Committee, Inc.	2	$2,250
Democratic Congressional Campaign Committee (DCCC)	3	30,000
Democratic Senatorial Campaign Committee (DSCC)	3	30,000
Democratic National Committee (DNC) Services Corporation/Democratic National Committee	2	30,000
Georgia Federal Elections Committee	2	3,000
Massachusetts Democratic Party	1	5,000
Minnesota Democratic-Farmer Labor Party/Federal	1	5,000
Nebraska Democratic State Central Committee	1	5,000
North Carolina Democratic Election Campaign Fund	1	2,500
Rhode Island Democratic State Committee	1	1,000
Tennessee Democratic Party	1	5,000
Republicans		
Georgia Republicans	2	2,200
National Republican Congressional Committee Contributions (NRCCC)	4	30,000
National Republican Senatorial Committee (NRSC)	2	30,000
New Hampshire Republican State Committee	1	200
New Jersey Republican State Committee	1	5,000
North Carolina Republican Executive Committee	1	2,500
Republican Federal Committee of Pennsylvania	1	500
Republican National Committee	1	15,000
Soft Money		
Democrats		
DCCC Nonfederal Account #1	8	20,500
DNC-Nonfederal-Corporate	11	246,704
DSCC Nonfederal Corporate	3	74,980
DNC Nonfederal Finance Fund	1	10,000
Republicans		
1995 Republican Senate/House Dinner Trust (Nonfederal)	3	32,000
1996 Republican Senate/House Dinner Trust and Building Fund (Nonfederal)	2	32,590
NRCCC-Nonfederal Account	3	35,250
NRSC-Nonfederal	3	106,000

Source: Compiled from Federal Election Commission data.

TABLE 3-7

Top Eleven Contributors of $150,000 or More to the National
Committees of the Democratic and Republican Parties

Contributor[a]	Industry	Democrats	Republicans	Total
Philip Morris	Tobacco	$496,518	$2,520,518	$3,017,036
Joseph E. Seagram & Sons	Liquor	1,261,700	677,145	1,938,845
RJR Nabisco	Tobacco	254,756	1,188,175	1,442,931
Walt Disney Co.	Media	1,063,050	296,450	1,359,500
Atlantic Richfield	Oil and gas	486,372	764,471	1,250,843
AT&T	Telephone	422,184	552,340	974,524
Federal Express	Transport	592,625	380,900	973,525
MCI Telecommunications	Telephone	607,296	357,218	964,514
Association of Trial Lawyers of America	Lawyers	606,300	197,100	803,400
Lazard Freres & Co.	Securities	624,500	163,100	787,600
Anheuser-Busch	Liquor	401,107	359,950	761,057

Source: Center for Responsive Politics.

Note: Figures are based on data obtained on-line from the FEC on 3 February 1997 and on data from the parties' year end reports filed on 31 January 1997.

[a] More than one contributor was affiliated with each organization.

"sold" the honor of sleeping in the White House in exchange for significant donations. Clearly, substantial soft money contributions are made in circumstances that facilitate communication between interest group representatives and policy makers.

Some interest groups contribute soft money to parties in an effort to boost party fortunes and influence electoral outcomes. Labor unions give to state Democratic parties to help elect Democrats to state and national office. Before making a contribution, COPE and other union PACs often insist that state parties show a coherent spending plan (Wilcox 1994). Party officials often direct soft money contributions to states where they believe such spending will be most effective or where an election is expected to be particularly close.

Many corporations, however, donate substantial amounts of soft money to both parties. Table 3-6 shows soft money contributions from AT&T PAC, which included a number of contributions to both political parties. Table 3-7 shows the major soft money donors in the 1996 election cycle. Tobacco companies lead the list, giving generously to both party committees. In an effort to maximize access for industry lobbyists, major executives from these industries may also give to both parties.

As discussed in Chapter 2, interest groups also help finance party conventions. In addition, they give to institutions that are affiliated with parties, that are not directly involved with elections, but that may ultimately help the party's electoral fortunes. For example, the GOP National Policy Forum helps identify and develop issues that Republican candidates can use in their campaigns. The forum is largely financed by interest groups, which contribute in order to gain access to important policy makers. The forum holds conferences where interest group representatives share their views with prominent members of Congress, including committee chairmen; in some cases, these conferences are held on the very day of major Senate or House committee hearings. Corporations that attend the conferences are usually asked to donate $25,000 (Marcus 1997a).

CONTRIBUTIONS OF GOODS AND SERVICES

Although most PAC contributions are simple cash transactions, PACs also contribute services, staff, and products—rather than money—to campaigns. Under FEC guidelines, in-kind contributions are subject to the same limit of $5,000 per candidate per campaign that applies to direct financial support. The worth of an in-kind contribution is estimated at fair-market value—that is, the price at which the candidate would have purchased the goods or services. If, for example, an interest group donates services worth $5,000 during a primary, it can give only $5,000 in cash or services during the general election. Approximately one in six active PACs in 1996 made in-kind contributions; nonconnected PACs and those associated with trade associations and membership organizations were the most likely to do so.

PACs make in-kind contributions for several reasons. First, such contributions enable a PAC to control how money is spent. PACs with electoral goals may be better able to help nonincumbents by providing a needed service than by giving them cash, which the campaign might spend on a less essential service. Second, a PAC may be able to produce some services below market cost, thus maximizing the use of its resources. Although a PAC may have only $20,000 in cash to give directly to candidates, it may be able to produce $35,000 in services to contribute instead. Third, because of the way that campaign law values certain in-kind contributions, they may be more valuable than cash.

One of the best bargains for a campaign is the donation of a poll. PACs that commission a number of polls can usually get them at a discount, and the value of the data turned over to the candidates varies with time. After fifteen days, a PAC can depreciate a poll by 50 percent; after sixty-one days, by 95 percent. Thus, a poll that costs $20,000 can be donated to a candidate for a value of only $1,000 after two months. In the final weeks of a campaign, such "old news" would be worthless—but early in a campaign, data even two months old can prove quite useful. In March of an election year, polls can warn incumbents of potential weaknesses or indicate the strength of a challenger's name recognition. In addition, polls can identify issues that are salient to voters in a particular district or state and help campaign committees determine how best to approach those issues.

The AMA is one of a number of organizations whose PACs lend the services of their pollsters to some favored candidates at a substantially discounted rate. AMPAC made more than $150,000 in in-kind contributions in the 1996 election cycle, including a number of polls. Larry Sabato (1984) reported that in one election cycle, AMPAC contributed polls that had cost $380,000, but because the polls were sharply depreciated, reported contributions of only $89,000. To guarantee contact between each candidate and AMPAC staff, AMPAC insisted that the candidate be personally involved in designing the survey and receiving the results. Moreover, AMPAC included some questions of its own on the surveys, which allowed the organization to absorb some of the costs and thereby further reduce the value of the contributions to candidates.

Although few corporate PACs provide surveys to candidates, BIPAC has recommended that corporate committees donate polls early in the election cycle, when they can help candidates develop campaign themes and positions on issues (BIPAC 1996, 12). Focus groups, another popular in-kind contribution in recent years, can also help candidates hone their message.

In addition to funding polls, interest groups make in-kind contributions by training and providing campaign staff. Membership organizations with ideological agendas—like the Sierra Club, the League of Conservation Voters (LCV), and the Human Rights Campaign (HRC)—are especially likely to provide volunteer support. According to Kim Mills, spokesperson for the HRC, that organization sponsors campaign training seminars for volunteers ages eighteen to twenty-five, then lends the trainees to key candidates. The group will even lend some of its full-time staffers to priority campaigns. In 1996, the HRC trained and dispatched twenty-five young adults to campaigns in eleven states and lent fifteen full-time staff members to campaigns in a dozen states. The LCV sent eighty volunteers and paid staff members to work for pro-environment candidates in targeted districts. This tactic provides a dual benefit: first, the interest group assists candidates who, if elected, will likely support its agenda; second, many trainees from successful campaigns are hired to work on Capitol Hill, earning long-term access to elected leaders and becoming potentially influential players in the legislative process. Some successful candidates have expressed gratitude for this kind of campaign assistance, as Democratic senator Mary Landrieu did in her 1996 election night victory statement when she singled out the HRC for the help it had given her campaign (Mundo forthcoming).

In 1996, the HRC held its own national political convention—"Outvote '96"—in Chicago between the dates of the national GOP and Democratic nominating conventions. At this event, campaign experts led training seminars on election tactics; after listening to motivational speeches, trainees were sent directly from the convention to their designated campaigns. The event attracted about 1,000 activists and included some prominent speakers— among them former White House counselor George Stephanopolous and Secretary of Housing and Urban Development Federico Peña.

Interest groups increasingly employ the services of political consultants and pollsters to test and develop messages and issue emphases. Such services can be shared with political campaigns and may influence how the candidates themselves choose and address policy issues. Perhaps most prominently, a number of conservative groups, including the Christian Coalition and the NFIB, financed research and polling in 1994 that led to the development of the Contract with America, the GOP's ten-point plan for policy change. The efforts of these groups helped to develop a national GOP message (including the Contract with America) and an agenda for the midterm congressional campaign. The groups benefited from having their principal issues articulated in the elections and can be given partial credit for the Republican takeover of Congress.

Interest groups can also provide candidates with targeting information to help them reach sympathetic voters (Herrnson 1994), training for candidates and campaign officials, and transportation for candidates. The variety of in-kind assistance that PACs can provide is vast, but since in-kind contributions require PACs to make a special effort to purchase or produce the goods or services and provide them to campaigns, by far the majority of active PACs do not engage in in-kind contributions.

SUMMARY

Although campaign contributions have occurred throughout history, contributions have varied in form because of changing fund-raising styles, changing technology, and—most important—changing laws. How funds from interest groups enter elections is currently determined by federal campaign finance laws passed in 1974 and 1979 and by a series of U.S. Supreme Court rulings that have overturned, modified, and clarified portions of these laws. This legal framework creates the opportunity structure for interest group involvement in campaign financing.

Interest groups make direct contributions as a means of communicating with candidates and party leaders. Indeed, most PAC and soft-money contributions are made at fund-raising events where interest group lobbyists have an opportunity to meet the candidate or party leader directly. Incumbents meet with PAC officials at breakfasts, cocktail parties, and dinners, and nonincumbents meet PAC officials when they can, often at events sponsored by party leaders or other patrons of the candidate. Some interest groups not only attend fund-raising events but also host them. A few set up events for nonincumbent candidates and invite officials from other PACs to attend.

Interest groups vary not so much in the way they make contributions as in who they choose to receive them: access-oriented groups are likely to give to committee chairs and party leaders regardless of whether they are in close elections, whereas electorally oriented groups give to candidates in close elections and try to channel their resources where they can make the largest impact.

Overall, however, interest group money for campaigns is mostly access money. The fact that most PAC money goes to incumbents makes elections less competitive. Challengers face long odds in any event, and these odds are made longer still by the fact that incumbents can raise money quickly by issuing invitations to fund-raising events that many PAC directors feel powerless to refuse.

For groups that hope to influence the outcome of an election, the limits on the amount of direct contributions to candidates pose a barrier to efficient allocation of available funds. A PAC with $300,000 to contribute cannot give all that money to candidates in two close races but is required by federal law to distribute it to at least thirty candidates.

In the next chapter we will focus on spending to influence voters—through issue advocacy, independent expenditures, and voter mobilization efforts—spending that occurs, in most cases, without any limits on the amount that can be directed to a particular race.

NOTES

1. Occasionally, candidates in southern states are involved in runoff elections; in such cases, individuals can give an extra $1,000.

2. A party or candidate that receives 5 percent of the popular vote in a presidential election is eligible to receive public funds in the next election. The public grant is equal to the percentage of the winning candidate's popular vote received by the candidate from the minor party. Thus, if the minor party candidate received 10 percent of the popular vote and the winning candidate received 50 percent, the minor party candidate would be eligible to receive a public grant in the next election equal to 20 percent of the grant awarded to the major parties.

3. Campaign finance information from the FEC is available at the commission's web site: http://www.fec.gov.

Other groups begin with FEC data, add their own research, and repackage the data for public consumption. For example, Citizens for Responsible Politics allows access to records from interest groups and their members at their web site: http://www.crp.org/index.html-ssi.

4. In this and the next chapter, "active" PACs are defined as those that both raised and contributed money in the election cycle.

5. Estimates provided to the authors by Robert Biersack of the FEC.

6. Calculations by the authors on the basis of FEC data.

7. To ensure that names on a rented list are solicited only once, many groups "salt" their lists with a few fictional individuals. A group or candidate that sends more than one mailing to the fictional group member has clearly violated the rental agreement.

8. An additional 12 percent received contributions but did not make contributions or independent expenditures.

9. PACs pursuing an electoral strategy sometimes become involved in primary elections. In the GOP, for example, interest groups on both sides of the abortion issue have mobilized behind their preferred candidates in intraparty contests. Other electorally oriented committees are active only in general elections, hoping to help their preferred party obtain the highest possible number of seats (Herrnson 1994).

10. The NRA is nonetheless overwhelmingly pro-Republican. In the 1994 cycle, the NRA contributed 4.7 times more to the GOP than to Democrats in House races and supported Republicans exclusively in Senate races ("Is the NRA 'Overrated?'" 1995).

CHAPTER 4

Interest Groups and Voters

Interest groups that pursue electoral strategies often try to persuade their members and other voters to support (or not to support) a particular candidate. They may communicate endorsements to their members or take out television and radio ads urging voters to support a specific candidate. They may distribute voters' guides in churches or outside welfare offices or mail them to their members with a letter urging them to distribute the guides in their neighborhoods. Such efforts are far more complicated than simply giving money to a candidate or party: a PAC contribution rarely involves more than writing a check and attending a cocktail party or a fund-raising dinner, but communicating with interest group members and other voters requires planning, production, and often careful research.

In the 1996 elections, interest groups mounted unprecedented campaigns on behalf of House and Senate candidates, in some cases spending more money than the candidates themselves. In special 1998 elections to fill seats vacated by the deaths of several members of Congress, issue advocacy campaigns dominated GOP primary elections. Such efforts allow interest groups to define the issues of a campaign and to frame the debate, a change that threatens to transform American elections from races centered on individual candidates to races centered on coalitions of interest groups.

In this chapter we examine how interest groups "get the word out" to their members and to the electorate at large. We begin by looking at the strategic context of interest group activity: the laws and common practices that create opportunity structures and the goals and resources that determine interest groups' strategies and tactics. The chapter then describes specific tactics in more detail.

THE STRATEGIC CONTEXT: REGULATIONS, GOALS, AND RESOURCES

Communication among interest groups and their members and other voters is regulated by tax law, by the Federal Election Campaign Act (FECA; discussed in Chapter 3), and by recent Court rulings on First Amendment rights.

Tax law limits the ways in which certain groups may engage in electoral activity, including the endorsement of candidates. Section 501(c) of the Internal Revenue Code permits organizations that promote the social welfare of the country to qualify for tax-exempt status. Groups that qualify for 501(c)(3) status can thus receive tax-exempt contributions, which is an enormous benefit because it allows wealthy benefactors to write off donations on their taxes. Moreover, 501(c)(3) organizations can receive large grants from foundations, which are banned from giving to groups that lack tax-exempt status. The 501(c)(3) groups cannot lobby Congress or engage in partisan political activity, but they are permitted to educate voters on issues and to encourage citizen participation in elections.

Organizations that do not qualify for 501(c)(3) status are often classified as 501(c)(4), which means that although they are not required to pay taxes on their revenues, contributions they receive are not tax deductible. Organizations classified as 501(c)(4) can engage in partisan politics, endorse candidates, and even sponsor a PAC, as long as political activity is not their primary purpose.

To protect their 501(c)(3) status, many citizens' groups do not issue formal endorsements; they nevertheless distribute information to their members (and to other voters) that makes it clear which candidate they support. The Christian Coalition, for example, does not officially endorse candidates, but its top leaders have appeared at partisan conventions as delegates for particular candidates and spoken candidly about their personal preferences, and the organization has produced voters' guides that left little doubt as to which candidate had the coalition's support. The Federal Election Commission (FEC) is seeking a ruling that would declare the Christian Coalition's campaign activities political advocacy.

When interest groups try to persuade voters to support or oppose particular candidates, they generally undertake either independent expenditures or issue advocacy. Both independent expenditures and issue advocacy were allowed by the Supreme Court's 1974 *Buckley v. Valeo* decision. PACs began to engage in independent expenditures soon after that decision, but case law on issue advocacy was not clarified until 1995—just in time for issue advocacy campaigns to explode in the 1996 elections.

Independent expenditures are defined as spending by a PAC or by an individual to advocate the election or defeat of a specific candidate. Such efforts must be genuinely independent and cannot be coordinated with the candidate or with a party committee. In the case of PACs, money for independent expenditures must be raised through contributions from members of the sponsoring group. Independent expenditures made by individuals or PACs must be disclosed to the FEC. The expenditures themselves are not subject to FECA contribution limits—there is no limit on the amount that a group or individual can spend in any single campaign or in all campaigns combined.

Issue advocacy is defined as spending that advocates particular positions on issues but not the election or defeat of particular candidates. Advertisements may mention candidates by name as long as they do not use specific words such as *vote for* or *defeat*. As is the case with independent expenditures, there are no limits to spending by interest groups or individuals in issue advocacy campaigns. In contrast to funds for independent expenditures, however, money for issue advocacy may come from interest group treasuries. Moreover, no disclosure to the FEC or any other agency is required.

Although it might initially appear that independent expenditures are a more effective tool for interest groups because they allow advertising campaigns that urge voters to elect or defeat specific candidates, fully 90 percent of issue advocacy ads in 1996 mentioned a candidate by name, and more than half included the candidate's picture. The ban on explicit endorsements is thus a minor hindrance. Ultimately, issue advocacy campaigns are less restricted because they allow interest groups to use funds not only from PACs but also from their treasuries and from member and nonmember donations. Perhaps most important, neither the activities undertaken nor the donor list need be disclosed to the government or media.

Why do interest groups go to such effort to communicate directly with voters? For groups that have broad policy goals and are seeking to influence the outcome of elections, direct communication with voters has several advantages over a simple campaign contribution. First, there are generally no limits on the amounts that interest groups can spend to communicate with voters, although there are procedural rules that affect just how the money is spent. If an interest group especially wants to influence the outcome of a single or a dozen House races, it can concentrate most or even all of its financial resources in those districts. Because the opportunity structure allows interest groups to contribute cash and spend money directly to influence voters, they can more efficiently target their money to races where it might make a difference.

Second, when interest groups communicate directly with voters, they control the content of the message, which enables them to more effectively mobilize their members and to highlight important issues among the larger electorate—and possibly to persuade some voters to support their position on those issues or to support candidates that they favor. Finally, direct communication with voters enables interest groups to put the candidate "on the record" in favor of their positions, which may make the candidate more likely to continue to support those positions in the future.

Consider, for example, television ads run by an environmental group urging support for a candidate who favors increased spending to clean up toxic waste sites. Members of the environmental group and other supporters of environmental causes are likely to respond well to this message, and many will be more likely to vote for the candidate. If the advertising is successful, district voters who are not members of the group may become increasingly concerned about toxic wastes; some may tell pollsters that more money should be spent on cleanup, and a few may even join the environmental group. If exit polls show that the candidate carried the environmental vote, the interest group's lobbyists may find it easier to gain access to the candidate if she is elected. Finally, by publicizing the candidate's promise to support increased spending on cleanup, the environmental group makes it more likely that she will actually follow through on this promise.

Interest groups use a variety of resources to communicate with voters. Groups with money buy television ads, groups with a large and active membership distribute voters' guides, and groups with prestige endorse candidates and allow the candidates, the parties, and other interest groups to disseminate the endorsement. Thus, even cash-poor groups can use non-cash resources to attempt to sway voting decisions.

Interest groups can choose among many tactics in their efforts to persuade voters to support or oppose a particular candidate. They can publicize the candidate's record or positions to the group's members, perhaps along with an endorsement. They can identify incumbents with—in their view—particularly undesirable voting records and publicize this information among group members, urging them to vote against the candidate. They can publicize voting records among the larger electorate by distributing voters' guides and by sending information to group members to distribute in their communities. Finally, they can fund radio or television advertisements urging voters to support or defeat a candidate, although some forms of advertising must take a more subtle approach.

ENDORSEMENTS

Many organizations will formally endorse a candidate to signal to their members which candidate best represents their viewpoint. Endorsements are first and foremost an attempt to persuade the membership to vote for the candidate, so they are inevitably distributed to group members, often by various means. The Sierra Club issues its endorsements for important national offices in its monthly magazine, and local chapter newsletters include these endorsements along with endorsements for state and local offices. Contributors to the club's PAC received special communications on the group's endorsements. Other organizations distribute endorsements on the Internet, through chains of members who receive and send faxed copies of endorsement lists, at local meetings, and through other channels.

Although endorsements may seem to be the most basic of all forms of interest group participation in elections, in fact, many organizations do not issue endorsements. A survey of interest groups by two political scientists found that only 8 percent of corporations, 9 percent of trade associations, and 29 percent of citizens' groups issued endorsements, although 95 percent of labor unions did so (Schlozman and Tierney 1986). Many corporations and trade associations made contributions to candidates without endorsing them, and some citizens' groups devoted considerable resources to electing candidates without issuing formal endorsements.

Why would a group give money and resources to a candidate but withhold a formal endorsement? Citizens' groups often refrain from endorsements because of limits imposed by tax law. But even among corporations, trade associations, and business groups that do not qualify as tax-exempt, endorsements are not common. Endorsements can create controversy within an organization: corporations and trade associations, for example, refrain from issuing endorsements in part to avoid long and contentious stockholders' meetings. An endorsement implies a high level of support from an organization, whereas a contribution from a PAC merely implies an ongoing relationship with a candidate.

The Endorsement Decision

Most organizations have a formal process for deciding whom to endorse, and the decision criteria are generally similar to those used for making contributions (discussed in Chapter 3). For incumbents, interest groups consider voting records; for nonincumbents, they consider any voting record in state or local government, answers to the group's questionnaires, and information provided by local activists. Many groups also assess candidates' viability and withhold their endorsement from those who have no chance of winning. To determine viability, larger and more complex organizations rely on committees and boards; smaller ideological groups often delegate the task to their director.

For example, WISH List (Women in the Senate and House)—a PAC that assists the campaigns of pro-choice GOP women—has a candidate review committee that serves under the board of directors. According to Executive Director Patricia Goldman, once candidates make themselves known to WISH List, the committee sends them questionnaires and schedules personal interviews with the most promising ones. On the basis of the questionnaire responses and the interview, the review committee makes a recommendation to the board. If the committee is split, the board makes the endorsement decision.

The WISH List committee and board assess two factors: first, whether the candidate shares the policy positions of the PAC; second, whether the candidate is capable of running a viable campaign. A candidate who is "right" on the issues but lacks political viability may not be endorsed. Groups such as WISH List—and EMILY's List, its Democratic counterpart—use their endorsements to signal to group members not only to vote for the candidate but also to contribute to her campaign; if the group endorsed candidates with no chance of winning, then group members would "waste" their money. Because group members trust the WISH List board to endorse only viable candidates, they feel confident making contributions on the basis of that endorsement. Pro-choice GOP women are thus especially eager to obtain the group's endorsement: they are aware that it will make fund raising easier and attract grassroots support. WISH List also publishes a regular newsletter featuring a selected list of endorsed candidates; this visibility is also sought by candidates, who recognize the value of publicity that reaches like-minded contributors and activists.

For the National Rifle Association (NRA) board that decides whom to endorse, the primary criterion is the candidate's voting record in public office. Tanya Metaksa, executive director of the NRA Institute for Legislative Affairs, notes that answers to questionnaires are helpful in making endorsement decisions but that candidates' actual votes on issues show what they will do "when the chips are down." Consequently, the NRA is most likely to support friendly incumbents, even when they are being challenged by candidates who are in nearly perfect agreement with NRA positions.

The national AFL–CIO has a general executive board made up of leaders from its eighty affiliated unions. According to Rudy Oswald of the George Meany Institute, a think tank devoted to studying labor issues, the board's endorsement in presidential campaigns is based primarily on candidate questionnaires and in some cases on appearances before the board, although not every declared candidate actually fills out a questionnaire or visits the board. For House and Senate races, decisions on endorsements begin at the local level and must be ratified by regional and then by state AFL–CIO councils. State recommendations for endorsements of House and Senate candidates are almost always honored by the national committee.

One side benefit of the endorsement process is the opportunity it provides for an interest group to force candidates to commit publicly to supporting the group's goals. Interest groups can make it clear that endorsements depend on public statements of support for or opposition to particular policies; groups may then create a record of a candidate's commitment, which can be used later by lobbyists when a measure is under consideration by legislators.

Contested Endorsements

Although endorsement decisions are often easy and straightforward, they sometimes provoke significant controversy within an organization. In the 1996 Massachusetts senatorial campaign between incumbent Democrat John Kerry and incumbent GOP governor William Weld, both candidates ran as social progressives who were proudly pro-choice on abortion. The National Abortion and Reproductive Rights Action League (NARAL), under some criticism for not reaching out to help pro-choice Republicans, debated its endorsement strategy and ultimately chose to favor Kerry.

According to James Wagoner, former vice president of NARAL, some members of the organization favored a neutral position to signal that both candidates were acceptable, but the organization's PAC board ultimately made a strategic decision to back the incumbent Democrat on the basis of two arguments: first, that Kerry was more likely to win, and second, that Weld would have to caucus with a GOP membership that leaned against abortion rights. Similarly, in a 1992 Senate race, the AFL–CIO was torn between incumbent Republican Bob Packwood and his challenger, Rep. Les AuCoin, a Democrat. Packwood had one of the best labor records of any Republican, but AuCoin was a stronger friend of labor. After much disagreement, COPE endorsed AuCoin, but some unions gave money to Packwood instead.

The dilemma faced by COPE—to support its strongest GOP ally or to endorse an even more loyal Democrat—is common to groups that attempt to maintain a bipartisan strategy. The Sierra Club currently operates under guidelines that require the endorsement of GOP incumbents with acceptable environmental records, even those who are challenged by a much "greener" Democrat. When faced with two friendly candidates, some groups endorse the incumbent, some use the occasion to increase the partisan balance of their endorsements, and still others select the candidate who most closely shares their views.

Endorsements may be especially contentious in social movement organizations, where activists may wish to display their anger at a candidate by withholding an endorsement. In March 1996, the board of the leading gay and lesbian rights organization, the Human Rights Campaign (HRC), decided to unequivocally endorse the reelection of President Clinton. It did so even though Clinton had eventually abandoned his pledge to allow gays and lesbians to serve openly in the military and had signed the Defense of Marriage Act—legislation widely perceived to be aimed specifically at denying rights to gay and lesbian citizens. The endorsement was highly controversial within the gay community, in part because many leaders believed that they could obtain stronger leverage with the White House by not issuing a formal endorsement so early in the campaign.

The HRC's decision to back Clinton did not signal total support for all of Clinton's actions on gay rights issues. The HRC had simply determined that Clinton was far better for its interests than any likely Republican nominee and that, overall, the president had made some real progress on gay rights. Furthermore, some members of the HRC board saw that the Defense of Marriage Act had been injected into 1996 election-year politics as a wedge issue to hurt Clinton, whose overall record on gay rights was better than that of any previous president. They accepted the fact that the president had signed the law with reservations rather than allow the GOP to force gay rights issues into the campaign. The HRC was able to make this compromise because it does not have any "litmus test" issues; in 1996, the organization also supported other candidates who had voted for the Defense of Marriage Act.

Americans for Democratic Action (ADA) endorsed Clinton in January 1996, despite widespread anger among the membership about the fact that Clinton had signed a Republican welfare reform bill that many ADA members believed would hurt poor Americans. ADA spokesperson Bob Corrolla called the endorsement a "pragmatic decision, given what had happened in 1994." He characterized this decision as a "defensive effort" to ensure against a conservative GOP Congress working with a Republican president. The Sierra Club also acted defensively and endorsed Clinton, despite his acquiescence to several antienvironmental riders pushed by the GOP Congress.

In contrast, although George Bush had been a lifetime member of the organization, the NRA withheld its endorsement in the 1992 presidential race because Bush had issued an executive order banning the import of some assault rifles. Nevertheless, several prominent NRA activists and officials personally endorsed Bush, privately bemoaning the ideological inflexibility that had led the organization to withhold an endorsement from the candidate who was clearly the least supportive of gun control. Later, in protest against NRA advertisements depicting agents of the Board of Alcohol, Tobacco, and Firearms as storm troopers, Bush publicly tore up his NRA membership card.

Perhaps even more controversial was the 1996 NRA decision not to endorse Bob Dole for president, even though Dole had a long-standing record of support for NRA positions. According to Tanya Metaksa, executive director of the NRA Institute for Legislative Affairs, once it had become apparent that Dole would be the GOP nominee, he began to try to moderate his image by abandoning his support for some crucial NRA positions. Metaksa said that even though Dole was more agreeable to the NRA than Clinton, supporting a candidate who had openly distanced himself from the group's positions had left the NRA no choice: "He set up a dynamic where it was impossible for us to support him because then we would be supporting someone who did not agree with us."

On occasion, interest groups will issue endorsements in contested primary elections, generally sparking heated controversy. In New York in

1992, two pro-choice Democratic women—Elizabeth Holtzman and Geraldine Ferraro—sought the Democratic nomination for the U.S. Senate to challenge incumbent Alfonse D'Amato, who at the time appeared quite vulnerable because of scandals. Holtzman and Ferraro, both former members of the House and rising stars in the Democratic Party, attacked each other throughout the campaign, eventually enabling state attorney general Robert Abrams to win the primary. In an action that deeply divided New York feminists, EMILY's List endorsed Ferraro, the Women's Campaign Fund endorsed both candidates, and the National Women's Political Caucus remained neutral in the primary (Rimmerman 1994).

Public versus Private Endorsements

Endorsements are generally intended to swing the votes of interest group members, but some organizations seek to influence nonmembers as well. Whether an interest group chooses to communicate its endorsements primarily to members or to publicize them further depends critically on how the group is perceived by the electorate at large. Popular organizations may seek to influence nonmembers by publicizing their endorsements, whereas more controversial groups may even attempt to keep their endorsements from the public eye.

Environmental organizations generally publicize their endorsements. Sierra Club political director Dan Weiss noted that "the Sierra Club is unique in that the endorsement is meaningful because the name means something. There is a noneconomic benefit to a Sierra Club endorsement. In effect, we offer the environmental version of the Good Housekeeping Seal of Approval" (Cantor forthcoming). Similarly, the League of Conservation Voters (LCV) issues an "Earth List" of legislators with the strongest environmental records, which is widely believed to influence environmentally minded voters who are not league members.

Organizations held in mixed regard may be forced to exercise caution with their endorsements. In the early 1980s, several pro-choice candidates asked NARAL to withhold endorsements because they feared mobilization by anti-abortion activists (Thomas forthcoming). Christian conservative groups have used endorsements from gay and lesbian rights groups to mobilize their members to help defeat candidates. Similarly, endorsements from Christian conservative groups often lead moderate and liberal voters to mobilize; in Virginia, for example, Democrats have successfully used Christian right endorsements of GOP candidates to persuade socially moderate suburban voters (including many Republicans) to support the Democratic candidate (Rozell and Wilcox 1996). Indeed, for a time, some Christian conservative organizations recommended that candidates deliberately hide endorsements and wage "stealth candidacies." The practice of concealing endorsements occurs most often at the local level, where some school board candidates allow endorsements to be disseminated in local churches but withhold them from the media.

Sometimes, organizations with opposing views may use the same endorsements simultaneously to mobilize their members. NRA endorsements, for example, are used to mobilize citizens who are for and against gun control. The net impact of an NRA endorsement appears to vary widely: in some states, it is almost always an advantage; in others, it often appears to be a liability. In some elections, such as in 1994, NRA endorsements helped candidates, while in elections that occur after highly publicized gun violence, NRA endorsements may ultimately be detrimental.

Endorsements and Voting Decisions

Do endorsements influence the voting decisions of interest group members? Generally, endorsements matter most among interest groups where membership is voluntary; members share common positions on particular issues and consider those issues central to their politics; and members trust the organizational leadership to evaluate candidates. Ideological interest groups—such as the Christian Coalition, NARAL, the NRA, the Sierra Club, and the National Association for the Advancement of Colored People (NAACP)—are the most likely to fit this profile. Endorsements probably matter most in House and in state and local races, where interest group members may have less information about the records and policy positions of the candidates than they do for national elections.

Although there has been little research on the value of endorsements, there is mounting evidence that they influence the votes of at least some members of interest groups. When endorsements are combined with voter mobilization efforts (discussed in a later section of this chapter), they can help swing close elections. For example, with the NRA at nearly three million members, many of whom are willing to base their votes on gun rights issues, an NRA endorsement can be an enormous asset to candidates in some regions. *Campaigns & Elections* reported that in 1994, the NRA had a substantial influence on the election of a GOP majority to Congress. Of the ten key NRA-backed candidates, nine won; of eleven key candidates that the NRA targeted for defeat, six lost (*Campaigns & Elections* Dec./Jan. 1995). Tanya Metaksa said that the group's involvement in the 1994 elections was the most extensive ever, with participation in over 10,000 races at all levels and an 82 percent success rate (Drew 1997, 41). Scholars have confirmed that NRA endorsements influence election outcomes (McBurnett, Kenny, and Bordua 1996).

One of the most important reasons that endorsements might fail to influence votes was articulated many years ago by David Truman in *The Governmental Process* (1951). According to Truman, membership in more than one group or interaction with members of other groups may subject voters to conflicting cues. Conservative gun owners, for example, may also belong to the Sierra Club and to a labor union, or they may talk politics with Sierra Club activists at NRA meetings, with union activists at the factory, and with liberal activists at PTA meetings. Rudy Oswald, of the George Meany Institute, points out that no interest group can simply assume that its endorsement will prevail with its members. A member of the AFL–CIO who is also a member of the NRA or of a conservative church-based group will be hearing very different messages about which candidates to support. Indeed, John Joyce, president of the 100,000-member bricklayers union, refused to endorse Bill Clinton in 1996 because Clinton's veto of the "partial-birth" abortion bill conflicted with Joyce's Catholic religious beliefs (Greenhouse 1996).

Ironically, although labor unions are more likely than any other type of interest group to issue endorsements, they do not fit the profile of organizations whose endorsements are most likely to carry weight. To begin with, labor union membership is not necessarily voluntary: in many states, certain places of employment are "closed shops," meaning that anyone who works there must join the union regardless of their political views. Although union members may share a common belief that management gives itself too many bonuses while underpaying the workers who make profits possible, they do not necessarily agree on abortion, affirmative action, welfare reform, or foreign aid. And in times of economic prosperity, union issues may seem less salient to workers than social, racial, and other issues. All of which suggests that union endorsements may not be especially effective in influencing workers' voting decisions.

Consider, for example, the 1984 presidential contest between Republican incumbent Ronald Reagan and Democratic challenger Walter Mondale. Reagan was the only president ever to have headed a labor union, but during his first term in office he dissolved the Air Traffic Controllers' Union and signaled to corporations that they could replace striking workers without fearing any action from the administration. Walter Mondale was such a longtime union ally that the AFL–CIO endorsed him during the primary elections and devoted a considerable amount of money and organizational muscle to helping him defeat Sen. Gary Hart from Colorado for the nomination. The AFL–CIO then endorsed Mondale in the general election with enthusiasm, as did nearly every other union in the country.

Meanwhile, Reagan used a variety of issues to target union voters: he sought the votes of inner-city ethnic whites by opposing affirmative action and taking a strong anticommunist stance, wooed workers by opposing welfare for those who would not work, and appealed to Catholic workers by opposing abortion and posturing on moral issues. Ultimately, 48 percent of members of labor union families voted to reelect Ronald Reagan as president in 1984 (Gallup Poll 1984): clearly, union endorsements failed to deliver a sweep of the labor vote to Mondale.

Although the 1984 election posed a particularly clear choice for union leaders, it was conducted during a time of rapid economic growth and job creation, when the "bread and butter" labor issues were less salient than emotional issues such as affirmative action, abortion, and defense—all issues that drive a wedge through the traditional Democratic coalition and lead some union members to vote for Republican candidates. Thus, in 1984, although ideological differences between the candidates and the strength of unions' endorsement of Mondale would have predicted a strongly Democratic labor vote, the circumstances of the election weakened the impact of the labor endorsement.

How do we determine the value of the unions' endorsement of Mondale? Reagan received 64 percent of the votes in nonunion households and 48 percent in union households—meaning that union households were 16 percent less likely to support Reagan than nonunion households. Although Mondale's comparatively stronger showing among union households may be attributable to union endorsements, many other explanations are possible: most union activists are Democrats, many live in urban areas, many are African American, and some are Catholic—all factors that predict a Democratic vote. The precise net impact of labor's 1984 endorsement of Mondale is impossible to determine, but it is likely that the endorsement itself swayed few votes.

In 1996, however, labor endorsements may have been more important. Although the 1996 elections were also conducted at a time of low unemployment, wages had been stagnant for some time. Moreover, labor lobby-ists had been shut out of the new GOP Congress: in a highly visible indi-cation of the changing attitude on Capitol Hill, the GOP leadership closed down the Capitol Building office that labor had used for years as its offi-cial outpost; in addition, the new House leadership directed GOP mem-bers not to meet with labor representatives. Early GOP initiatives on union issues worried many rank-and-file workers, and union leaders succeeding in using GOP actions to mobilize union members.

HIT LISTS

In addition to endorsing some candidates, interest groups may single out others for defeat. The "hit list" is generally thought to have originated with Environmental Action, which in the early 1970s created the "Dirty Dozen"—a list of legislators with the worst environmental records. The familiar and catchy phrase drew more negative attention to candidates than would any straightforward listing of those with environmentally unfriend-ly voting records. In the course of five election cycles, Environmental Action included fifty-two different incumbents on its list, and twenty-four were defeated in the years they were listed (Schlozman and Tierney 1986). Today, the Dirty Dozen list is issued by the League of Conservation Vot-ers, which uses the hit list to target electoral efforts. In the final two weeks of the 1996 election, the LCV spent heavily, using independent expendi-tures to run 472 television and 382 radio advertisements in efforts to defeat targeted candidates (Gugliotta 1996).[1] Phillip Mundo reports that the LCV Action Fund uses both the "Earth List" and the "Dirty Dozen" to make resource allocation decisions (Mundo forthcoming).

In 1996, the AFL–CIO targeted 104 members of Congress for defeat, 45 of whom—including 11 GOP House freshmen—lost their elections (Herrnson 1997). Other organizations, including feminist and environ-mental groups, also identified candidates whom they felt had especially poor records on important issues.

Interestingly, being placed on a "hit list" can sometimes become an asset to a targeted candidate. In 1996, the HRC conducted its first-ever inde-pendent spending campaign against a candidate, openly targeting North Carolina Republican senator Jesse Helms for defeat. The HRC spent about $250,000 against Helms, assisted with phone banks and literature drops, and contributed the services of several staff members to assist challenger

Harvey Gantt's Democratic campaign. Given his long-standing hostility toward gay rights and his sometimes vitriolic statements about homosexuality, Helms was a logical first target for this organization. But in a state that is largely culturally conservative, Helms carried opposition from the gay community as a badge of honor and believed that he gained more than he lost from the organized opposition.

For a variety of reasons, hit lists are far less common than endorsements. First, the leaders of many interest groups believe that if their organizations concentrate on hit lists, they will be perceived by the media and the political community as excessively negative. Second, hit lists greatly antagonize incumbents, most of whom are likely to win reelection and become even more energetic in opposing the interest group's agenda. For groups pursuing either legislative or electoral strategies, hit lists run the risk of decreasing access to important policy makers. Finally, some groups that tried to target incumbents with negative campaigns in the 1980s got strong feedback from group members who disapproved of the tactics and threatened to withhold support in future elections.

RATINGS, SCORECARDS, AND VOTERS' GUIDES

Like endorsements, ratings, scorecards, and voters' guides enable interest groups to provide convenient voting cues to members and the public alike. Ratings and scorecards evaluate legislators' support for an interest group's agenda, usually by listing votes on important bills and amendments and summarizing that information as a numerical score that ranges from 0 to 100 percent support. Ratings, which generally provide longer and more complex evaluations of incumbent votes, are aimed primarily at activists, lobbyists, and journalists; scorecards, usually shorter and simpler, are aimed primarily at interest group members. Voters' guides present candidates' positions on issues of concern to interest groups and their members.

For interest groups that claim or seek a 501(c)(3) tax status, ratings, scorecards and voters' guides allow the group to influence the voting decisions of their members and the broader electorate without specifically endorsing candidates.

Interest groups (such as the AFL–CIO and the Sierra Club) that endorse candidates may also issue ratings, scorecards, and voters' guides. Ratings and scorecards provide more nuanced information than a simple endorsement:

although an organization may endorse two candidates for separate seats in the House, for example, one may have a 100 percent score and the other a 60 percent score; ratings and scorecards thus clarify for interest group members the precise extent to which each candidate has supported the group's policies. Such a signal can sometimes influence fund raising by the candidate among interest group members and sympathetic PACs. Moreover, ratings can help interest groups' lobbyists: informing a member of Congress that an upcoming vote is going to be a part of the next scorecard may provide an extra incentive to support the group on the issue in question.

The National Farmers Union was the first group to use the legislative scorecard, in 1919 (Hrebenar 1997, 187). The oldest continuous congressional voting record has been maintained by Americans for Democratic Action (ADA), which first issued a scorecard in 1947. The scorecards of the ADA and the American Conservative Union (ACU) both include a wide variety of issues designed to assess candidates' general ideology, and the ADA and ACU ratings are often used by political scientists to measure the liberalism and conservatism of members of Congress. For many years, in order to attract greater publicity. and influence voting decisions, the ADA and ACU released their scorecards in a joint press conference after Labor Day each election year.

Some interest groups evaluate candidates' positions on a range of issues in a single domain. The Family Foundation of Virginia, for example, rates state legislators' "family-friendly" votes on issues that range from sex education to abortion to tax rates. In the 1980s, the Christian Voice issued the "Morality Scorecard," which attracted widespread attention and derision when it was revealed that the group had given some ordained religious leaders scores of 0 and awarded scores of 100 to some House members who had been convicted in the Abscam corruption probe or censured for sexual affairs with teen-age pages (Wilcox 1992).

Most interest groups rate candidates on a narrow set of issues of special interest to the group's membership. The LCV describes its National Environmental Scorecard as "an annual report card on how Congress votes on the environment" (Mundo forthcoming). The National Federation of Independent Businesses (NFIB) rates legislators according to roll call votes on bills affecting small business. The HRC scorecard for the 104th Congress rates legislative votes on "issues of particular concern to lesbian and gay voters" (Human Rights Campaign 1996).

The National Committee to Preserve Social Security and Medicare (NCPSSM) rates legislators on their votes on issues "having the greatest effect on seniors' health care and retirement income" (National Committee to Preserve Social Security and Medicare 1996). The votes may have been taken on final passage of legislation, on amendments, or on procedure. For the 104th Congress, NCPSSM devised a rating scale based on representatives' records on eleven crucial votes, such as the Medicare Preservation Act of 1995. The scorecard included a brief explanation of each of the eleven issues that the House voted on and then identified the organization's formal position (in favor or opposed). For each vote, the group gave each member of the House either an R (for voting right) or a W (for voting wrong). A representative who voted "right" ten times out of eleven, for example, received a 91 percent positive rating from the group. NCPSSM also listed cumulative scores for each member of Congress, indicating the percentage of correct votes in all legislative sessions dating back to the group's founding in 1983.

Scorecard measures depend critically on which votes are selected for counting: if ten or fewer votes are counted, the selection of two roll calls can change an incumbent's score by 20 percent or more. In some cases, interest groups deliberately—sometimes quite transparently—manipulate the ratings to inflate or deflate candidates' scores. In early 1996, the Christian Coalition released a congressional scorecard that gave incumbent GOP senator John Warner, Va., a 100 percent rating. Yet several months later, challenged in a GOP primary by the more conservative James Miller, Warner suddenly found himself with only a 23 percent favorable rating from the Christian Coalition's voters' guide. After Warner won renomination and was challenged by a pro-choice Democrat, the coalition issued a new voters' guide that focused on different issues and gave Warner an 86 percent positive rating (Rozell and Wilcox 1997).

Like endorsements, legislative scorecards do not always have the positive impact hoped for by the organization that issues them. Candidates sometimes use positive ratings from particular groups to mobilize voters against their opponents. Southern Democrats, for example, often find it difficult to defend a high ADA score. Nevertheless, scorecards do signal to interest-group members and others sympathetic to their goals precisely which incumbents are the most supportive, enabling them to target their resources to those candidates.

Ratings and scorecards generally rate all incumbent members of the House and Senate on selected roll call votes on bills, amendments, and motions of concern to the organization. Voters' guides differ in several ways. First, they provide information on the policy preferences of incumbents and nonincumbents alike. Second, they are generally tailored to particular electoral constituencies: Wyoming voters, for example, would receive a guide rating presidential, Senate, and House candidates in that state; voters in Montgomery County, Maryland, would receive similar information about presidential candidates, but the information about Senate and House candidates would apply only to their jurisdiction. Finally, voters' guides are usually distributed a few days before an election and are designed to be taken into the ballot box to guide voting directly.

Although voters' guides are presumably nonpartisan efforts to distribute information about candidates' positions, they provoke controversy because they sometimes contain misleading information. In the 1994 Virginia Senate campaign, despite Democratic incumbent Charles S. Robb's support for the "Helms amendment" to cut federal funding for "offensive art," a Christian Coalition voters' guide characterized Robb as favoring funding for "obscene art." Robb had voted for a federal budget package that included funding for the National Endowment for the Arts, and included in that package was funding for art that many social conservatives considered offensive. Of course, many conservative senators also voted for the federal budget, and in states where the coalition supported conservative candidates who had voted for the budget, it did not characterize them as supporting "obscene art." The Christian Coalition distributed some 1.7 million voters' guides in the Virginia Senate race alone (Rozell and Wilcox 1996).

The 1996 Christian Coalition voters' guides listed eight to ten issues, depending on the district, including late-term abortions, gun control, and the balanced budget amendment. The guides were strategically worded to elicit an electoral outcome favorable to the group. In one case, the guides used the phrase *federal firearm ban* to refer to a congressional vote on banning semiautomatic weapons; this phrasing made it appear that candidates who supported a ban on semiautomatic weapons were also opposed to recreational hunting weapons, regardless of whether this was the case (People for the American Way 1996).

The Christian Coalition claims to have distributed 67 million voter guides in the 1996 elections, primarily in churches attended by at least one member of the group. Some 45 million were distributed the Sunday before the election, leaving candidates little time to respond to the descriptions of their positions (Rozell and Wilcox 1997).

The Interfaith Alliance, created to help mobilize moderate and liberal Christians, distributed five million of its own voters' guides in some forty congressional districts. In 1996, the Interfaith Alliance decided which congressional races to emphasize on the basis of how active the Christian Coalition was in those districts. Executive Director Gregg Lebell explained that a major goal was simply to challenge the credibility of the Christian Coalition's voters' guides. In addition to issuing its own alternative guides, the Interfaith Alliance sent letters to approximately fifty thousand ministers in the targeted districts alerting them to potential legal problems created by the distribution of Christian Coalition guides in churches.

Interest groups often target their voters' guides to districts and states with close elections. Labor '96, an effort led by the AFL–CIO, distributed voters' guides in targeted congressional districts in the final month of the campaign. The issues emphasized in the guides were based on polls and focus group interviews with labor union members. Like the Christian Coalition guides, the labor guides compared candidates' positions on crucial issues, leaving no doubt as to which candidate had labor support. Intended primarily to help mobilize pro-labor voters, the guides carried the headline "What's at Stake for Working Families in the 1996 Elections?" (Gerber forthcoming).

VOTER MOBILIZATION

An interest group's impact on an election is a function of its size, its voting cohesion, and its participation rate. Even small groups can influence elections if their members vote in every possible election and vote together, whereas even large groups can have little influence if their members stay at home on Election Day. Thus, when interest groups communicate with their members and supporters—through voters' guides, for example—they are seeking not only to influence voting decisions but also to increase turnout at the polls.

Groups that can effectively "deliver their members" are sought after by parties and candidates trying to assemble electoral coalitions. Moreover, such groups can often use the cohesiveness of their membership as a lobbying asset. For example, when NRA leaders first approach a new member of Congress, they may tell her the number of NRA members in her district. The intent is to convey that many NRA members base their voting decisions primarily on gun rights issues and NRA endorsements. A simple membership count would thus indicate to a new House member that the NRA can help deliver those votes to her—or to her opponent— in the next election and that her degree of support for NRA issues could swing many votes.

Like endorsements and ratings, voter mobilization efforts sometimes have unanticipated consequences. The coordinated efforts in the 1960s to mobilize black voters in the South succeeded impressively, but white turnout increased at a similar rate (Rosenstone and Hansen 1993). In many states, voter mobilization efforts by the Christian right have caused countermobilizations by moderate suburbanites, helping Democratic candidates to win elections (Rozell and Wilcox 1995). Nevertheless, such countermobilizations are often less enduring than the effects of sustained efforts by interest groups to politicize their members. Steven Rosenstone and John Mark Hansen (1993) argue that voter mobilization efforts by social movement organizations succeed because they lower the costs of participation and increase the benefits. Voters' guides and endorsements reduce the information costs of the voting decision, and getting in touch with members and telling them when and where to register and vote reduces the information costs of the voting act. By creating a network of social expectations, voter mobilization efforts increase the benefits of voting as well.

In addition to undertaking voter mobilization, many groups attempt to recruit activists to participate more broadly in elections—to volunteer their time and money on behalf of candidates, to work within their social networks and communities to persuade friends and acquaintances to support candidates, and to perform many other tasks that benefit candidates and parties. The usefulness of this tactic depends not on how many members an interest group has but on the size and devotion of its activist core.

Tactics

Many electorally oriented interest groups make special efforts to mobilize members, and distributing voters' guides is part of that process. When interest group members see a stark contrast between two candidates on issues that matter to them, they may be more willing to take the time to vote. Many groups, however, go beyond distributing voters' guides and reach out to members with direct appeals to participate. A week before the elections, the NRA distributes a bright orange 3 x 5 endorsement card as a reminder to its members—a tactic that the group's executive director for legislative affairs calls one of its most effective communication tools. (See Figure 4-1.)

A highly innovative approach to communicating to interest group members and supporters was the 1996 Interfaith Alliance "voter's pledge." Modeled after the candidate pledges (for example, not to raise taxes) of

FIGURE 4-1
NRA–PVF Endorsement Card

NH Exec. Council

*NRA-PVF ENDORSES PETER GAMBLE
FOR GENERAL ELECTION

Dear NRA Member: October 28, 1996

On **Tuesday, November 5,** the general election will be held for Executive Council. Your vote to elect **Peter Gamble** is vital to preserving both our Second Amendment rights and our hunting heritage in New Hampshire.

At a time when attacks on our rights by anti-gun elected officials have never been stronger, fellow NRA member, **Peter Gamble** can be counted on to defend our rights as a member of the Executive Council. It is important that New Hampshire gun owners and sportsmen stand behind friends like Peter Gamble so that they can fight for the law-abiding citizens of New Hampshire.

YOUR VOTE CAN MAKE THE DIFFERENCE. Take this card with you to the polls on Tuesday, November 5, and cast your vote to elect **Peter Gamble to the New Hampshire Executive Council.**

Sincerely, Tanya K. Metaksa, Chairman, NRA-PVF

* The NRA Political Victory Fund is NRA's political action committee.

Source: Used with the permission of the National Rifle Association of America Institute for Legislative Action.

other organizations, the Interfaith Alliance pledge asked voters to commit to taking the elections seriously by studying the issues, learning the candidates' positions, and actually voting. The goal of the pledge was not merely to provide a public service by asking people to focus on the elections, but more directly to help turn out voters who shared the organization's faith-based moderate and progressive views.

Most often, interest groups reach voters by telephoning them. The Christian Coalition claimed that its volunteers made millions of phone calls to remind Christian conservatives to vote (Toner 1997), and labor unions generally organize phone banks in districts and states with close elections, calling union members and their families and encouraging them to participate. Many other interest groups call selected members before an election and urge them to vote.

Interest groups with an active membership base rely on volunteers to staff phone banks and sometimes to transport members to the polls. A few groups simply have a computer dial a list of phone numbers and play a recorded message. Although there are no hard data to prove it, most observers believe that a personal phone call is far more effective than a recorded one. Some groups mail glossy reminders and sample ballots to members in carefully targeted districts, and a few are beginning to experiment with Internet (e-mail) reminders to vote.

Interest groups that have strong attachments to particular parties often try to mobilize not only their own members but also other potentially sympathetic voters. To increase turnout among voters likely to support Democratic candidates, the voter mobilization efforts of Labor '96 included a special focus on senior citizens and minorities (Gerber forthcoming). Christian Coalition voter mobilization efforts are often conducted through churches, where volunteers distribute information and talk about the election with church members who are not part of the group.

Churches provide a special forum for voter mobilization efforts because they are full of active individuals who share common beliefs and always have a meeting two days before an election. Both Christian conservative groups and liberal civil rights groups make a special effort to recruit ministers, who can be instrumental in mobilizing voters. In the black community, churches often mount voter registration drives, and on the Sunday before Election Day, pastors inevitably exhort their members to vote, often for particular Democratic candidates. In recent years, white evangelical churches have become the locus of voter mobilization efforts as well. In the early 1980s, the Moral Majority mounted voter registration drives in fundamentalist churches; and in 1988, many Pentecostal pastors encouraged their members to participate in the GOP primaries and caucuses in support of Pat Robertson. In 1994, National Election Study data showed that 25 percent of white evangelicals and 22 percent of black Protestants said that they had been contacted in their churches by someone who encouraged them to vote.

Financing

Voter mobilization efforts often involve creative financing, with money transferred freely between interest groups, political parties, and special voter mobilization projects. Special ad-hoc, "nonpartisan" voter mobilization projects can receive tax-exempt contributions from individuals and organizations as long as they do not advocate the election of specific candidates. An example of a truly nonpartisan voters' drive is Rock the Vote, a group formed in 1992 with the goal of mobilizing young voters, who are notoriously apathetic. In that election year, the group relied primarily on concerts, mass rallies, and targeted television advertising on youth-oriented programs to deliver its message. By 1996, the group had started a voter registration service with a toll-free phone number (1-800-REGISTER) paid for by MCI. Callers simply provided the voice-mail message service with their address and zip code and requested registration information; a little over a week later, they received a pre-stamped envelope and completed registration form that required only their signature. Rock the Vote and MCI then started an Internet voter registration site that also allowed for simplified registration. The week before the national elections, voters who registered through either service received a postcard reminding them to vote ("The Youth Vote" 1996).

Because most voter mobilization efforts are officially nonpartisan, they are not permitted to focus on just one party or candidate. In practice, such efforts often subtly (or not so subtly) help one party or candidate more than another—for example, by targeting precincts where most voters are likely to support candidates of one party. In 1996, labor gave $2 million and lent staff assistance and expertise to nonpartisan voter registration projects working primarily in districts targeted by the AFL–CIO. Democratic voter mobilization efforts might be centered in poor inner-city areas with substantial minority populations, and GOP projects might be focused in rural white areas of the South. These special voter mobilization projects are often created unofficially by the political parties, but they can also be sponsored by particular candidates. In 1986, Democratic senator Alan Cranston of California created a voter mobilization campaign headed by his son. Charles Keating, head of a failed savings and loan association that was seeking special intervention to help deal with regulators, contributed more than $1 million to that effort.

Interest groups can contribute money to other interest groups that are mounting voter mobilization campaigns or can coordinate with those groups and provide them with goods and services. The National Committee for an Effective Congress (NCEC) specializes in producing studies that help candidates and interest groups target their resources to maximum benefit. The NCEC shares its information with Democratic Party officials, with special voter mobilization projects, and with the AFL–CIO and other liberal groups to enable them to more successfully reach likely Democratic voters.

Moreover, political parties may contribute money to interest groups in an effort to mobilize voters. The *Washington Post* revealed that the Republican National Committee (RNC) steered millions of dollars in contributions from its major donors to sympathetic organizations, including the

National Right to Life Committee and Americans for Tax Reform. The largest contribution went to the American Defense Institute, which runs voter mobilization campaigns for military personnel (Marcus 1997b). Toward the end of the 1996 election cycle, the RNC gave large donations to these three groups—including more than $4 million to Americans for Tax Reform—to help mount get-out-the-vote drives. Current law allows parties to make such contributions to interest groups as long as the party and the group do not coordinate their activities. In practice, large contributions to interest groups' voter mobilization efforts can serve as clever devices for parties, enabling them to accomplish their electoral goals without being subject to restrictions on the use of the money.

Coalitions

Just as individuals become more effective political actors by forming groups, groups become more effective by forming coalitions. If a single interest group mobilizing its base of supporters is a formidable force in electoral politics, a collection of groups is that much more so. Some coalitions are formal, featuring their own letterheads with a list of member groups: the Long Term Care Campaign, for example, conveys the strength of its numbers by listing all 143 member groups on its letterhead.

But an informal coalition of groups can be every bit as influential, perhaps even more so. When asked to identify the most formidable grassroots coalition in the country, many elected officials and interest group representatives immediately cite the "Leave Us Alone" coalition, and many cite its director, Grover Norquist, as the most formidable grassroots organizer in America. Norquist's coalition has no formal place of business, no letterhead, no list of members. No one can look it up in a phone book or in a Washington directory of lobbyists. Norquist maintains that he prefers the flexibility afforded by anonymity: it allows him to oust groups should they become "coalition-unfriendly" (Drew 1997, 6).

The Leave Us Alone coalition is a collection of conservative groups that generally believe in limited government, although not all agree on its meaning. The coalition includes leaders and members of such groups as the American Association of Retired Persons, the U.S. Chamber of Commerce, the Christian Coalition, the Eagle Forum, the Heritage Foundation, the National Right to Life Committee, Republicans for Choice, the Small Business Survival Committee, property rights groups, and home-schooling groups.

Although the members of the coalition have clear differences on certain issues, they agree to put them aside when working together to help conservative candidates get elected to public office. As Norquist explained to reporter Elizabeth Drew:

> If everyone in the room can agree—the gun owners agree not to throw condoms at the Christian kids, and the Christian groups agree not to steal anybody else's guns, and the small business groups agree not to raise anybody else's taxes, and the tax groups agree not to take other people's property—as long as everybody agrees not to screw with anybody else—everyone's happy. And everybody can leave and spend the rest of the day crushing the left. It's a low-maintenance coalition (Drew 1997, 6).

The coalition's tactics are quite straightforward: interest group leaders meet regularly to discuss strategy and then go back to their own groups to mobilize their memberships. During the 1996 campaign, Elizabeth Drew had access to the coalition's regular Wednesday morning meetings, and she weaves a fascinating story of how Norquist and others developed plans for mobilizing the grass roots. In one meeting, the day after the New Hampshire primary, representatives from about seventy groups discussed strategy for the rest of the campaign. Dismayed by the victory of conservative commentator Patrick Buchanan, who many feared would cost the GOP its control of Congress, coalition members agreed to cooperate throughout the campaign to prop up GOP House members and challengers in competitive races.

Some coalitions form during one election and then disband altogether or until the next election cycle. For example, the Labor '96 effort included a broad-based coalition of generally liberal-leaning organizations working to increase turnout among sympathetic voters. Coalition members included the Asian-Pacific American Labor Association, Citizen Action, the Coalition of Labor Union Women, the Interfaith Alliance, the National Baptist Convention, the National Rainbow Coalition, Rock the Vote, the A. Phillip Randolph Institute, and the Women's Vote Project. A recent study of Labor '96 describes one component of the coalition effort:

> Working Women Vote was organized by the new Working Women's Department of the AFL–CIO. Their efforts resulted in three hundred events, including rallies, conferences, bus tours, precinct walks, leafleting, mailings, registration drives, and phone banks in forty-six states. They coordinated with thirty international unions and twenty nonprofit groups to get a total of 35,000 activists involved in the election (Gerber forthcoming).

In election years, interest groups often work together to push politically charged issues onto the legislative agenda. This strategy increases the likelihood that particular policies that the groups supports will become law; alternatively, if the proposals do not pass, coalition members are better able to use the issues to mobilize their own groups in the election. In 1996, labor groups pushed hard for enactment of an increase in the minimum wage—legislation unlikely to emerge from a GOP Congress. But the proposal was enormously popular, and under the implicit threat that unions would be able to mobilize their membership and appeal to the larger electorate over this issue, many Republicans voted for the bill, which passed and was signed by the president. Similarly, in 1996, social conservative groups—betting that President Clinton would issue a veto—pushed for enactment of the Defense of Marriage Act; their strategy was to inject the issue of gay rights into the campaign and provoke a massive mobilization of social conservatives at the polls. Despite reservations, the president signed the bill—a decision few believe he would have taken in a nonelection year.

INDEPENDENT EXPENDITURES
AND ISSUE ADVOCACY

Under the tax laws, activities classified as voter mobilization must be non-partisan efforts to encourage citizens to participate in elections and are not permitted to show or recommend support for specific candidates and issues. To persuade their members and other citizens to elect or defeat a particular candidate, interest groups must use other means—principally, independent expenditures and issue advocacy.

Independent Expenditures

PACs have made independent expenditures in support of candidates since 1976, when a Supreme Court ruling allowed them to do so. Ideological groups discovered the efficacy of the technique in 1980 and began using it effectively. In the 1980 New Hampshire presidential primary, Republican candidate Ronald Reagan benefited from more than $250,000 in independent expenditures undertaken by the Fund for a Conservative Majority—spending that some observers credited with helping Reagan prevail in that "must win" election. In the 1980 general election, the National Conservative Political Action Committee (NCPAC) targeted for defeat a number of Democratic House incumbents and six Democratic senators who had voted in 1978 for the Panama Canal Treaty. NCPAC spent more than $1 million in advertising in those races, airing commercials that attacked the incumbents on issues such as government spending, defense spending, and abortion. One advertisement against Idaho's Frank Church aired throughout the state 150 times daily for five weeks (Schlozman and Tierney 1986, 216).

The impact of NCPAC's spending was the subject of some debate. Four of the six targeted senators lost, indicating that NCPAC's barrage of ads may have weakened support for some of the incumbents. Yet it is also likely that many would have lost regardless of NCPAC's involvement. In each case, the incumbent ran well ahead of Democratic presidential candidate Jimmy Carter, but Ronald Reagan carried the states and districts of the losing incumbents by a landslide. In this strongly Republican year, liberal Democrats were vulnerable, as eight other Democratic incumbents lost.

In 1982, NCPAC again targeted senators and House members it considered liberal, but in the depths of a recession the Democratic candidates fared quite well. In one case, Maryland Democratic senator Paul Sarbanes attacked NCPAC for interfering in Maryland politics. When Sarbanes's comments led to a gain in the polls, his Republican challenger asked NCPAC to pull its ads.

By 1984, NCPAC was deeply in debt to its direct-mail fund raisers, and although it claimed to have spent millions in independent expenditures to help reelect Ronald Reagan, most of this reported spending was for overhead and for mailings to its members asking for more money. NCPAC eventually declared bankruptcy after the death of its founder, John "Terry" Dolan.

NCPAC's brief moment in the sun raised many fears about the role of independent expenditures in elections. Dolan made extravagant claims about the power of his organization, claiming at one point that NCPAC "could elect Mickey Mouse to the House and Senate," and bragging that his group could issue false statements in its advertising without tainting the candidate—because the candidate would have had nothing to do with the ad. Indeed, many of NCPAC's ads distorted the truth or ignored it entirely—claiming, for example, that senators had cast particular votes when in fact they had cast the opposite vote or no vote at all; characterizing anti-abortion Democrats as pro-choice; and thoroughly distorting the policy positions of many candidates (Sabato 1984; Schlozman and Tierney 1986).

Although ideological groups like NCPAC and the National Right to Life Committee have received the greatest attention, some of the most effective and concentrated independent expenditure campaigns have been waged by large trade associations such as the American Medical Association (AMA) and the National Association of Realtors (NAR). In California in 1986, the AMA spent $252,199 on behalf of Republican David Williams, who was challenging incumbent Democratic representative Pete Stark. The Williams campaign itself spent only $61,483, which meant that the AMA was able to say far more about Williams than was Williams himself. The NAR also engaged in independent spending in the 1980s, although the organization has since stopped such activities (Bedlington 1994, forthcoming).

In 1996, PACs spent more than $10 million to advocate the election or defeat of candidates for federal office. More than 90 percent of this money was spent by nonconnected, trade, and membership PACs. For some non-connected PACs, however, total independent spending was exaggerated. The National Right to Life Committee, for example, listed staff salaries, travel costs, and other expenses as independent expenditures, even though the group would have incurred such expenses regardless of its involvement in election campaigns. In some cases committees are required by law to item-ize such expenditures on behalf of candidates. Nonetheless, at least some spending by nonconnected PACs did little to influence electoral outcomes.

Many independent expenditures, however, did fund formidable advertis-ing campaigns for competitive House and Senate races whose outcomes interest groups hoped to influence. In 1996, more than $400,000 was spent for and against Randall Tate in Washington state, for example. A religious conservative and Newt Gingrich ally, Tate had won election in 1994 with only 52 percent of the vote. Tate benefited from independent expenditures made by the AMA, the Coalition for a Drug-Free America, the NRA Polit-ical Victory Fund, and the National Right to Life Committee. Tate's Demo-cratic challenger, Adam Smith, benefited from significant independent expenditures made by the LCV's PAC, the National Council of Senior Cit-izens, Voters for Choice and Family Planning, and Planned Parenthood. Tate lost the election narrowly, and went on to head the Christian Coalition.

The focused spending in the Tate race points to an important feature of independent expenditures in 1996. Although the bulk of PAC contributions went to incumbents who were in no danger of losing, the overwhelming majority of independent expenditures were concentrated in close races. In 1996, less than one-third of PAC contributions went to House candidates involved in close elections, whereas nearly all (99.7 percent) of independent expenditures were targeted to close races (derived from Herrnson 1997, 117, 122). Similarly, 99.1 percent of independent spending in Senate races was targeted to close elections. Clearly, interest groups seeking access to

Congress prefer to make direct contributions, whereas groups seeking to influence elections often engage in independent expenditures.

Issue Advocacy

Although issue advocacy was allowed by the Supreme Court in 1976, it was not until the 1990s that its legal limits were articulated by circuit courts. In 1996, the Supreme Court distinguished between speech that is "express advocacy," which includes exhortations to vote for a particular candidate, and speech that merely advocates particular positions on issues. In 1991, the First Circuit Court allowed the Maine Right to Life Committee (MRLC) to distribute voters' guides that included (1) candidate and party positions on abortion, (2) information on whether a particular vote was consistent with the position of the National Right to Life Committee, and (3) a statement claiming that the publication did not represent an endorsement of any candidates. In addition to allowing the distribution of the guides, the circuit court allowed the MRLC to use corporate revenues to finance publication of the voters' guides.[1]

In 1995, the Fourth Circuit Court upheld a lower court ruling that a 1992 advertisement funded by the Christian Action Network did not expressly advocate the defeat of Bill Clinton.[2] The ad opened with a full-color picture of Bill Clinton's face

> superimposed upon an American flag, which is blowing in the wind. Clinton is shown smiling. As the narrator begins to describe Clinton's alleged support of "radical" homosexual causes, Clinton's image dissolves into a black and white photographic negative. The negative . . . gives Clinton a sinister and threatening appearance. . . . The commercial then presents a series of pictures depicting advocates of homosexual rights . . . demonstrating at a political march. . . . As the scenes from the march continue, the narrator asks in a rhetorical fashion, "Is this your vision for a better America?". . . The narrator then states, "for more information on traditional family values, contact the Christian Action Network" (advertisement cited in Potter 1997, 234–235).

This court decision and others like it opened the way for interest groups to spend millions of dollars on advertising and other efforts that were clearly designed to support or attack specific candidates but that avoided using the "magic words" that constitute express advocacy. Early in the 1996 election cycle, the AFL–CIO announced plans to spend $35 million on issue advocacy in carefully selected House districts where newly elected GOP representatives might be vulnerable to defeat. The organization initially targeted 75 House Republicans, eventually expanding that number to more than 100 (Herrnson 1997). In an advocacy campaign that was coordinated with voter mobilization efforts by labor and with the grassroots activities of many other organizations (Gerber forthcoming; Herrnson 1997), the AFL–CIO spent $25 million to air 27,000 television commercials in 44 House districts and distributed more than 11 million voters' guides comparing Democratic and Republican stances without explicitly endorsing candidates.

One ad that ran in the district of George Nethercutt, a Republican freshman who had defeated House Speaker Tom Foley in 1994, featured the weathered faces of several older citizens and the following voice-over:

> Congressman George Nethercutt voted to cut our Medicare benefits.
> George Nethercutt knows it. And so do we. Fact: on November 17, 1995,
> Nethercutt voted with Newt Gingrich to cut $270 billion from Medicare
> funding, while voting for tax breaks for the wealthy. Now he's trying to
> deny it. Tell George Nethercutt we know the truth about his vote to cut
> our Medicare benefits. Another vote is coming. This time, we'll be watch-
> ing (Sack 1996b).

Other ads tried to increase support for labor positions in the general electorate. Although it is unclear whether such efforts affected public perceptions, a study by the Annenberg Public Policy Center noted that one highly publicized strike in early 1997 was the first time in many years in which the public sided with the union, and Republican members of Congress appeared somewhat more hospitable to labor after the 1996 election (Beck et al. 1997).

When the AFL–CIO announced its plans for a massive issue advocacy campaign, the NFIB began planning a counterattack. Urged on by GOP party chair Haley Barbour, the NFIB joined with the U.S. Chamber of Commerce, the National Association of Manufacturers, the National Restaurant Association, and the National Association of Wholesaler-Distributors to form "The Coalition: Americans Working for Real Change." Eventually, about thirty business groups joined the coalition, which spent some $5 million to air approximately 6,000 television and 7,000 radio advertisements.

Although these expenditures were far lower than those of the AFL–CIO, the coalition had the advantage of knowing where and when AFL–CIO ads were to air so that it could counter them, sometimes defensively (Shaiko and Wallace forthcoming). Here, for example, is the voice-over text from one coalition advertisement:

> Election year. There'll be a lot flying through the air. But when you look through the mud, you see what Congressman ___ has helped to achieve: the first real cuts in spending since World War II. Two hundred and seventy wasteful government programs eliminated. Historic welfare reform that requires recipients to work for their benefits. Why should we ever go back to the past? When you see the mud, remember the accomplishments. Call Congressman ___ and tell him to keep reforming our government (Beck et al. 1997, 29).

The coalition was one of many ad-hoc organizations formed specifically to undertake issue advocacy campaigns, primarily for Republican candidates. Citizens for Reform, for example, was a Virginia-based tax-exempt organization formed in 1996 by Peter Flaherty, a conservative Republican activist. In October and November of 1996, Flaherty's organization spent some $2 million to air advertisements focusing on issues such as term limits and the balanced budget amendment. Some ads, however, addressed various aspects of candidates' personal lives, a move that seemed to stretch the idea of issue advocacy to its limits; while the group claimed for tax purposes to be addressing issues and not candidates, some ads were clearly designed merely to attack candidates. In Montana's deadlocked House race, for example, Citizens for Reform ran the following advertisement: "Who is Bill Yellowtail? He preaches family values, but he took a swing at his wife. And Yellowtail's explanation? He 'only slapped her.' But her nose was broken" (*Los Angeles Times,* 5 May 1997; cited in Beck et al. 1997).

Like many other conservative groups formed specifically to undertake issue advocacy, Citizens for Reform was a client of Triad Management. The role of Triad in forming several issue advocacy groups—and in channeling money from major donors to these groups—has sparked controversy and ongoing investigation. Billing itself as a "contribution advisory service" for conservatives, Triad advised many conservative donors to contribute funds to two groups that, in turn, financed commercial broadcasts and mass mailings. In the final few weeks of the elections, Triad's efforts funneled about $3 million in donations from undisclosed sources into advertising alone. Triad and the affiliated groups defended the advertisements as issue advocacy, noting that because the ads did not explicitly advocate the election of any Republican candidate, they were perfectly legal (Gugliotta and Marcus 1997).

Issue advocacy has also sparked other controversies with observers questioning the factual accuracy of some advertisements and suggesting that sponsoring organizations may be pushing the boundaries of fair, ethical, and perhaps even legal campaign practices. Intending to send a chilling message to older Americans that a GOP-led Congress would eliminate Medicare, the AFL–CIO broadcast advertisements in 1996 quoting House Speaker Newt Gingrich, R-Ga., bragging that the program would eventually "wither on the vine." The GOP maintained that the ad had distorted Gingrich's statement by taking it out of context. The National Republican Congressional Committee, charging that the ad was "defamatory," sent warning letters to all broadcast stations running it. Nineteen television stations and nine radio stations lifted the ad, but about fifty other broadcast stations disregarded the warning. The AFL–CIO responded first by defending the accuracy of the ad, then by increasing its media buys in markets that continued to run the ad (Clymer 1997).

In 1998, issue advocacy played a key role in a special primary election in California. The primary involved two Republican state legislators competing for their party's nomination in a House district vacated by the death of Rep. Walter Capps. Although the primary occurred in a moderate-leaning district, the wealthy centrist candidate lost to a Christian social conservative who had been supported by a $100,000 ad campaign conducted by an anti-abortion group (Cannon 1998); the Christian conservative candidate subsequently lost the general election to Capps's widow. This example suggests that issue advocacy may be especially important in primary elections: the strong anti-abortion advertisements appear to have influenced conservative voters in the GOP primary. In the general election, however, anti-abortion issue advocacy may well have sparked a counter-mobilization among pro-choice citizens.

Controversy over the factual accuracy of issue advocacy campaigns is one aspect of broader concerns—namely, candidates' inability to control either the themes or positions articulated in such campaigns. A 1997 Annenberg Public Policy Center study estimated that in the 1996 elections, some thirty-one interest groups spent between $135 and $150 million on issue advocacy advertisements, along with additional funds for brochures, voters' guides, and other materials to be distributed by members (Beck et al. 1997). Nearly all of this money was spent in a few dozen targeted races. The combined financial power of issue advocacy and independent expenditures often meant that the candidates could control neither the issues under discussion nor the themes of their campaigns.

In Pennsylvania's twenty-first district, for example, interest groups and party committees together spent more than $1.4 million on issue advocacy campaigns promoting the election or defeat of one candidate or the other, whereas Republican incumbent Phil English spent $1.2 million and Democratic challenger Ron DiNicola only $468,000. Both candidates complained that they were sometimes blindsided by advertising promoting their candidacies in ways that they did not approve of (Gugliotta and Chinoy 1997).

The barrage of issue advertising that characterized the 1996 elections seems likely to be repeated in future election cycles; indeed, most observers predict that such spending will increase. This possibility troubles many analysts and public officials, who argue that our traditional electoral system, in which candidates selected their own campaign themes, articulated their own positions, and defended their own advertisements, is in danger of being overwhelmed by issue advocacy, in which coalitions of interest groups attack and defend candidates using images and words for which the candidates can deny responsibility. Sen. Max Cleland, D-Ga., has lamented that under the current system, "candidates and campaigns become pawns in an election game directed by outside interests" (Cleland 1997). Moreover, a number of the organizations that undertake issue advocacy campaigns appear to be ad-hoc groups assembled primarily to channel money from wealthy donors into targeted congressional races. These groups have no members per se, and their funding sources remain obscure. Cleland points out that, in contravention of the intent of the FECA and its amendments, "money in many campaigns is not coming primarily from accountable people, but from unaccountable, unfamiliar groups" (Cleland 1997). We will return to the concerns raised by issue advocacy campaigns in the concluding chapter.

REFERENDUMS, INITIATIVES, AND RECALLS

Many citizens are increasingly put off by traditional political parties and their candidates, but interest groups have discovered that they can mobilize voters by creating opportunities for them to vote directly on issues of concern. A direct popular vote—through a referendum, initiative, or recall—is an increasingly popular, albeit controversial, way for interest groups to mobilize their members and other voters.

Although interest groups place referendums on the ballot for many reasons, the most important is the opportunity to bypass state legislatures and governors and write the group's policy preferences directly into law—to expand or contract civil rights protections for gays and lesbians, to protect or restrict abortion rights, to favor one type of automotive insurance over another. Referendums serve other purposes, however, and interest groups sometimes place them on the ballot even when they are sure to lose. Referendums can (1) mobilize group members to become more politically active, (2) help groups recruit new members, (3) provide a forum to help persuade the public on an issue, and (4) increase voter turnout in other races that are also on the ballot.

In the 1996 elections, a record number of ninety state ballot initiatives appeared in the twenty-four states that permit the use of the procedure. In thirteen of the states, the initiatives included term limit proposals; other issues ranged from banning clear-cutting in Maine's North Woods to dismantling affirmative action programs in California.

In some states, such as California, ballots typically include a long—sometimes numbing—list of initiatives. In 1996, for example, the California State Board of Elections sent every voter a book over two hundred pages long explaining all the ballot initiatives. Because only the most highly motivated voter is likely to have the time and energy to become informed on so many issues, many voters fail to vote on any initiatives. Thus, ballot issues are often decided by a relatively small percentage of those who actually voted—a circumstance that strengthens the ability of organized groups to influence policy development directly. Among those most likely to have sufficient interest and inclination to vote on ballot initiatives are members and supporters of interest groups that have a stake in the outcome.

In some cases, ballot initiatives are controversial and high-profile events that attract even more interest than election races. In 1996, most observers considered the outcome of the presidential race in California predictable, and Bob Dole's Republican campaign even left the state for a time. Nor did the more competitive California congressional races receive much attention. Instead, all eyes seemed to be turned to a highly controversial state ballot initiative, Proposition 209, that would dramatically change the state's affirmative action laws. The initiative passed comfortably, although challenges to its constitutionality continue.

In Colorado, Amendment 17, a so-called parental rights initiative, attracted substantial national attention and sparked battles between national interest groups. Some viewed the initiative as protecting parents' basic rights from government intrusion; others regarded it as potentially providing legal protection for child abuse. Led by the Christian Coalition, conservative Christian groups campaigned for the referendum and vastly outspent their opposition, a coalition of 150 Colorado-based groups led by

People for the American Way. The referendum ultimately failed, with 57 percent of Colorado voters opposed.

Ballot initiatives can sometimes result in unlikely political alliances. In 1994, the Idaho Citizens Alliance, a conservative Christian group, succeeded in placing on the ballot a proposal to limit gay rights. Although the group reached out to conservative leaders and activists as well as to citizens in the more conservative rural communities, it found itself squarely opposed by business leaders (who believed that the initiative would reflect poorly on the image of the state and damage the business climate) and by potato farmers (who feared a nationwide boycott of their famed product if the initiative passed). Conservative business people, potato farmers, and gay rights groups worked together against the ballot initiative.

The initiative ultimately failed, but its presence on the ballot may have influenced election races. Rep. Larry La Rocco, D-Idaho, who lost his seat that year to a very conservative candidate by about 20,000 votes, attributes his loss in part to the ballot initiative, which actually drew a majority in his district and succeeded in mobilizing a large number of social conservatives who then voted for his opponent. Indeed, interest groups may work to put issues on the ballot as a means of marshaling activists who will then vote for the group's preferred candidates.

For many groups, the major challenge in promoting an initiative is meeting all the requirements to get on the ballot. State laws allowing initiatives to be placed on the ballot vary dramatically; in many cases, the number of signatures required is so large that interest groups have begun hiring firms that pay workers to collect signatures. In California in 1996, Common Cause and the League of Women Voters worked with other public interest organizations to collect the required 700,000 signatures for a campaign finance initiative, hiring firms that were ultimately responsible for collecting about one-half of the signatures. The state director of Common Cause said that to have been able to collect as many as one-half of the needed signatures through volunteers was an outstanding achievement, noting that interest groups in California typically paid for most of signature collection (Tollerson 1996).

Paying for signature collection is controversial because the principle behind the popular referendum is that an issue with substantial grassroots support—but perhaps lacking the clout that comes with big money—can have a chance at success through direct popular vote. A large base of volunteers, intense enough in their beliefs to invest time and effort in collecting the required number of signatures, is strong evidence of an issue's popularity and legitimacy. With paid signature collection, however, moneyed interests have a substantial advantage in using the initiative process to promote their agendas.

SUMMARY

Interest groups with large memberships or well-stocked treasuries frequently try to influence election outcomes by communicating with their members and other voters in efforts designed to help specific candidates. Although tax law forbids some interest groups from endorsing candidates, the law is sufficiently vague and enforcement lax enough to enable most groups to find ways to communicate their preferences to members and other voters. Moreover, spending on such activities is often unregulated, meaning that it can be financed by interest group treasuries and need not be reported to the FEC.

Issue advocacy—the latest form of direct communication with voters— became a major strategy for interest groups in the 1996 elections and in the special elections of 1998. Issue advocacy troubles many scholars and policy analysts, who see the potential for American elections to be transformed from candidate-centered contests to battles between competing coalitions of interest groups. Moreover, issue advocacy introduces into elections an element of uncertainty that is of concern to well-funded incumbents, who may find their substantial war chests dwarfed by interest-group spending in their state or district. Similarly, party leaders have begun to worry about the impact of issue advocacy on party primaries. Finally, corporate America is busy promoting state laws to ban political spending by labor unions—a move that would leave corporations free to spend unmatched millions on issue campaigns. In the final chapter, we take up the normative issues raised by these and other activities and discuss possible campaign finance reforms.

NOTES

1. *Federal Election Commission v. Faucher,* 928F.2d 468 (1st Cir.), cert. denied, 502 U.S. 820 (1991).

2. *Federal Election Commission v. Christian Action Network,* 92 F.2d 1178 (4th Cir. 1996).

CHAPTER 5

Evaluating the Role of
Interest Groups in Elections

Chapters 2, 3, and 4 described the myriad ways in which interest groups participate in elections—from grassroots mobilization to cash and in-kind contributions, from recruiting and training candidates to conducting independent expenditure and issue advocacy campaigns. This concluding chapter addresses two questions: First, what are the advantages and disadvantages of interest group involvement in elections? Second, how might reforms improve the ways in which interest groups are involved in elections, and thereby also improve the ways in which American elections are conducted?

ADVANTAGES AND DISADVANTAGES

There is little agreement among political scientists, journalists, or even interest group activists about the role of interest groups in elections. At one extreme, interest groups can be viewed as pure democracy in action: aggregating the voices of individual Americans, articulating their concerns, drawing them into the electoral system, and raising money to finance candidates' campaigns. Most observers who offer an unqualified defense of interest group involvement in American politics argue that although short-term disturbances may temporarily favor one group or set of groups, competing forces will mobilize to redress imbalances, and the interest group universe will achieve balance over the long term. Others reject the notion that balance is a goal: in their view, the participation of interest groups in electoral processes embodies the basic freedoms of American democracy—speech and the right of assembly—and any regulations, including those already on the books, are infringements of individual liberty.

At the other extreme are those who believe that almost every aspect of interest group involvement in politics is damaging to the electoral process. According to this view, when interest groups seek nominations for their own members, they usurp the power of parties. When they create advertisements to sway the larger electorate, they usurp the role not only of parties but also of the candidates themselves. When they help finance elections, they buy or "rent" members of Congress, influencing the content of legislation in ways that may be harmful to the nation as a whole. When they endorse candidates, they create misleading and oversimplified messages and distort incumbents' records, often sponsoring "attack" advertising campaigns that increase public cynicism and decrease voter turnout. Finally, when interest groups place ideological purity above all else, they undermine the pragmatic compromise that is the bedrock of American democracy.

In sum, analysts and observers who are concerned about interest group participation in electoral politics see it as the embodiment of the factionalism that James Madison feared. Many view the interest group universe as highly unbalanced—dominated by corporate America or by corporations and unions, each out for its own financial gain. Critics note that although many Americans are not members of interest groups, their voices go unheard, drowned out amid the shouting of interest group activists.

Few people take such extreme positions, of course. We believe that there is some truth to what both defenders and critics of interest groups have to say. In our view, the current and evolving role of interest groups has positive and negative implications for the conduct of American elections and for democracy more broadly. To get a closer look at these implications, we will reconsider the major activities covered in Chapters 2, 3, and 4: communication with parties, with candidates, and with voters.

Interest Groups and Parties

Although interest groups and social movements have long been active in American political parties, today this activity is more visible—and perhaps more vitriolic—than ever before. Political scientists differ greatly in their evaluations of the role of interest groups in American political parties, with some arguing that interest groups help democratize parties and others contending that they eviscerate them.

One positive consequence of interest group involvement in party affairs is that the recruitment process has become more inclusive, drawing into the candidate pool many Americans who might never have sought office before. For example, many talented women, African Americans, and conservative Christians have become candidates, expanding the scope of demographic and issue representation.

Of course, in political systems where parties control nominations, it is possible to make even more rapid progress toward the inclusion of outgroups. In 1997, the British Labour Party increased the number of women Labour candidates from 138 to 159, boosting the number of Labour women members of Parliament from 37 to 102 and doubling the proportion of all women MPs to 18.2 percent (Lovenduski 1997). In the United States, however, without the active involvement of women's groups, the system of party primaries and caucuses would make it more difficult to increase the numbers of women in Congress.

When interest groups contend for influence in parties and create more vigorous competition for party offices, the party leadership is less likely to be a static, "inbred" group that may have lost touch with the larger electorate (Baer and Bositis 1993). The ability to infuse new life into party elites is especially important because party leaders in the United States resisted the inclusion of blacks in the Democratic Party, women in both parties, and Christian conservatives in the GOP.

In addition, by mobilizing members of previously apolitical or disenfranchised groups—drawing them into political parties; encouraging them to seek nominations as delegates to local, state, or even national conventions; helping them to run for party office; enlisting them to work to influence party platforms—interest groups help develop the political skills of their members and increase their capacity for participation in democratic processes. Many union workers, African Americans, women, and Christian conservatives who are active in party politics today may have started without the socioeconomic background and resources that are generally associated with political activism, but their involvement in interest groups enabled them to develop the skills needed for politics.

Finally, by compelling debate on party platforms, interest groups sometimes force parties to confront important issues they might prefer to ignore. Promoting debate within parties is especially important in the American political system: in European multiparty systems, policy debates are often conducted among the political parties; because we have a two-party system, internal party debates and disagreements become all the more important. For example, when members of the civil rights movement began working within the Democratic Party, party officials and candidates had to confront racial inequality, an issue that both parties had been more comfortable ignoring. Similarly, although abortion clearly evokes intense feelings in many Americans, the heated debate among Republicans on abortion would not have occurred without the perseverance of the Christian right.

Despite these advantages, interest groups can also do significant damage to political parties. Chapter 2 discussed several instances in which social movement organizations worked to nominate unelectable candidates and saddled other candidates with platforms that brought intense and derisive media attention. At times, interest groups can fragment parties into contending factions: in Virginia and Minnesota, for example, survey data show that the moderate and Christian right factions are extremely antagonistic, rating each other's candidates and leaders below even those of the Democratic Party. Indeed, both moderates and conservative Christians surveyed in Virginia found that assigning a score of 0° on a "feeling thermometer" was not enough to signal their dislike of the other faction; some penciled in scores of −10,000°, along with some nasty marginal comments (Rozell and Wilcox 1996). And thus far, the internal GOP debate on abortion has been more of a shouting match than a genuine policy debate, with Christian conservatives repeatedly trying to deny moderates party office, party funding, or access to the ballot, and many Republican moderates leaving the party in protest against GOP nominations of social conservatives.

Political scientists have written extensively about the rule changes that opened up the presidential nomination process to active involvement by ideological groups. In the 1970s and early 1980s, many analysts felt that social movement organizations had hijacked the nomination process: because the new procedures favored ideological groups and candidates at the expense of party regulars and moderates, the parties often nominated "outsider" candidates who were either unelectable or unable to govern effectively once elected. Critics held further that interest groups had usurped traditional party functions such as recruitment, nomination, and the development of party platforms, always to the detriment of the parties (Broder 1972; Ceaser 1979, 1982; Polsby 1983).

Although we agree that there is some truth to these arguments, we think that they are overstated. Clearly, the system in place since the early 1970s has not always produced ideologically extreme candidates who cannot win or govern competently. In the fourteen party nominations since the 1972 reforms, the Democrats have produced only one ideologically extreme candidate—George McGovern—who did indeed lose more convincingly than virtually any other Democratic nominee would have. The Republicans also produced one—Ronald Reagan—who went on to be the first president since Eisenhower to serve two full terms.

Critics have charged that in the Democratic Party, the new open system led to the nomination of Walter Mondale, who was too liberal for the electorate. But Mondale—a party regular and former vice president who had done well in nationally televised debates—would likely have been the party nominee even under the old rules: he was exactly the kind of "insider" who, according to critics of the 1970s reforms, could not have been nominated under an open, participatory system. Moreover, Mondale was probably less liberal than his mentor, Hubert Humphrey, who won nomination under the old system, and may have been closer to the political center than his opponent, Ronald Reagan. With the nation at peace and the economy in the midst of a rapid, short-lived recovery, it is unlikely that any Democratic nominee could have defeated Ronald Reagan.

Jimmy Carter is also frequently mentioned as a product of the new rules, but his nomination was not due to the involvement of interest groups; instead, voters flocked to Carter because he was an outsider to the system, and Johnson, Nixon, Ford, and Agnew—all products of the old closed system—had disappointed the electorate. Thus, Carter's election may owe as much to the failures of leaders nominated under the closed rules as to the new open rules. It is worth noting that in the 1990s, the new open system nominated George Bush, Bob Dole, and Bill Clinton—all three moderate candidates with considerable political experience; the old system, in contrast, produced Barry Goldwater, whose extreme rhetoric at the 1964 convention led to a coordinated walkout by party moderates.

Overall, interest group involvement in the internal life of parties can lead to more vibrant and inclusive party organizations but it can also divide parties into contentious, uncompromising factions. We join with many other political scientists in preferring a system with stronger parties than now exists in the United States, although we also value the role of interest groups in creating a more diverse and representative system and in raising important issues on the political agenda.

Political parties are private associations, and they can change their rules to limit or expand the role of interest groups in internal party politics. For example, although Republican moderates face an uphill battle against Christian conservatives, it would be possible to create a stronger national party organization and to give that organization more control over the selection of state and even local party chairs. Such changes are unlikely, however, in the American political culture, especially given the GOP's long-standing support for local autonomy.

Interest Groups and Candidates

Direct contributions from interest groups to candidates and parties constitute the most controversial aspect of American elections. Critics of the current system routinely charge that political action committees (PACs) sponsored by interest groups have "bought" politicians, parties, or even all of government: a book by a prominent advocate of reform was entitled *The Best Congress Money Can Buy* (Stern 1988). One astute observer of Congress argues that "PACs are probably the primary source of cynicism and distrust of politics in the United States today" (Wright 1996, 115).

For many nonincumbent candidates, interest group resources are essential to launching their campaigns. Nonincumbent candidates must often invest large amounts of their own money (Wilcox 1988), but interest groups can provide crucial resources at this stage, contributing the "seed money" that helps nonincumbents get their campaigns underway (Biersack, Herrnson, and Wilcox 1993). EMILY's List, WISH List (Women in the Senate and House), and the Gay and Lesbian Victory Fund all contribute and bundle money to nonincumbents early in the campaign, helping many promising candidates win election.

Moreover, interest group money enables candidates to get their message out. Although critics charge that Americans spend too much on elections, in fact we spend less on national, state, and local election campaigns than we do marketing consumer products such as beer and toilet paper. Ours is a complicated political system: voters must sort out differences not only between parties but also among candidates, a task that requires a great deal of information. By providing services to help candidates develop their messages and by providing funds to help them articulate and deliver their messages, interest groups play a valuable and important role in a privately funded political system.

Finally, by encouraging their members to give to PACs and to candidates that their group supports, interest groups provide members with an additional avenue for political participation. Although contributing is a specialized form of participation that does not automatically lead to greater political involvement, it is nonetheless a form of participation (Verba, Schlozman, and Brady 1995). Many women who would never have considered becoming politically active have joined EMILY's List or WISH List and now attend fund-raising dinners and meet candidates. Similarly, corporate and business PACs seek to engage the interest of executives who might otherwise tune out politics.

Nevertheless, the role of interest groups in financing elections is not all positive. Because PAC contributions go primarily to incumbents, they render American elections less competitive. Incumbents begin with a long list of advantages—name recognition, political contacts, and the perquisites of office, among others—but PACs have enabled them to enjoy a tremendous fund-raising advantage as well.

Critics often charge that PAC contributions do more than help incumbents win reelection: they also buy incumbents' votes, or at least "rent" their policy making power for a time. More recently, watchdog groups such as Common Cause and the Center for Responsive Politics have argued that large contributions of soft money from interest group treasuries have led to specific policy payoffs in recent federal budgets.

In *Return on Investment: The Hidden Story of Soft Money, Corporate Welfare, and the 1997 Budget and Tax Deal,* Common Cause (1998) charged that soft money donations to both parties led to a series of specific provisions that appeared, after no debate, in budget and tax bills. The report charged that Amway Corporation, which helped fund the 1996 Republican National Convention and gave more than $1 million in soft money to the GOP in the first six months of 1997, benefited from a provision that changed the rules for determining whether assets in foreign subsidiaries are passive investments and therefore subject to taxation. Designed principally for Amway, the provision gave the company a huge tax break. Similarly, tobacco companies initially benefited from a budget provision holding that revenues from a tax hike on tobacco would be used to pay off any settlement the industry negotiated with some forty state governments over tobacco-related health costs. Public outcry eventually led Congress to repeal this provision, although without media efforts to stir up public outrage, it would have become law. The Common Cause report quotes Kenneth Kies, staff director of the Joint Committee on Taxation, as saying that "the industry wrote it and submitted it and we just used their language." As we saw in Chapter 3, tobacco interests are among the largest contributors of soft money to both parties.

Major donors of soft money sometimes acknowledge that they give money in an effort to influence public policy. In 1997, businessman Roger Tamraz cheerfully admitted before a Senate committee that he had given more than $300,000 in hard and soft money contributions to various Democratic Party committees in an unsuccessful effort to influence a policy decision by the Clinton administration. When asked what he might do differently next time, Tamraz replied that he might give even more money, since $300,000 was apparently insufficient to buy the policy he preferred. In 1986, more money was given by Charles Keating, head of a failed savings and loan association, to five Democratic and one Republican senator in an effort to persuade them to intercede with federal regulators on his behalf. Although some of these senators, most notably California Democrat Alan Cranston, did meet with regulators, ultimately Keating did not receive regulatory relief.

The failure of Tamraz and Keating to win the policies they sought points to the difficulty of determining just what large and small donations buy for those who make them. Numerous studies by political scientists have found that PAC contributions have only a small impact on roll call votes by members of Congress, which suggests that contributions may swing a few votes on some bills but seldom influence enough votes to make a significant difference (for example, Chappell 1982; Grenzke 1989; Welch 1982; Wright 1985, 1996). Nevertheless, insider accounts of policy making often focus on the importance of money. Why does political science research indicate that PAC money has only a small influence on policy, while insider accounts portray money as having a large impact?

Political scientists and political activists have reached different conclusions for several reasons. First, critics who have observed a simple relationship between PAC contributions and votes have assumed that this pattern inevitably implies that money bought political support. But PACs give to members of Congress not only to try to gain access to influence policy but also to reward past support. Consider, for example, the fact that anti-abortion PACs routinely give money to anti-abortion House member Henry Hyde, R-Ill., who has fought abortion throughout his House career. A simple comparison of PAC contributions and votes shows that Hyde received four contributions from anti-abortion PACs in 1996 and was a strong supporter of the ban on "partial-birth" abortions in that session. Yet these facts do not mean that anti-abortion PACs "bought" Hyde's vote—or that if pro-choice PACs would simply give him more money he would switch his vote. Instead, it means that some of the statistical relationship between PAC contributions and roll call votes arises because PACs give money to members of Congress who already support them—even if those members would likely support them without a contribution.

Political scientists first try to determine how a member of Congress might have voted had he or she not received a PAC contribution—on the basis of influences such as personal convictions; constituents' views; arguments and pressure from colleagues, party leaders, and the president; and arguments and pressure from interest groups. In some cases where a PAC contribution matches a roll call vote, there are other explanations for the vote. Often, an interest group is successful at lobbying members of Congress because it represents large numbers of voters in a state or district or because other important political players support the group's views. The tobacco industry, for example, could gain access to senators and representatives from North Carolina or Virginia even without contributing to their campaigns, simply because it employs many voters in those states and the income of those voters indirectly supports many other businesses. Thus, the apparent relationship between PAC contributions and roll call votes is more complex than it may seem to political activists.

Moreover, many political scientists believe that because incumbents are able to raise large sums of money from many sources, even a coordinated effort by a major industry generally amounts to a small portion of donation receipts. For example, Chapter 3 noted that Virginia Republican senator John Warner had received more than $200,000 in PAC contributions from the defense sector and more than $70,000 in individual donations from executives and their families in the defense industry. Yet Warner raised more than $1.5 million in PAC contributions in that election cycle and more than $2.2 million in individual contributions of more than $200. Having contributed less than 10 percent of Warner's campaign totals, the defense industry was scarcely in a position to demand that Warner deliver any specific policy benefit. Any single PAC likely accounted for less than 1 percent of Warner's total funds. In most relationships between PACs and incumbents, it is the incumbent who is more powerful.

In sum, one of the reasons for the discrepancy between the observations of political scientists and those of some critics who are concerned about PACs is that the critics do not appear to take into account the complexity of the relationship between PACs and incumbents. At the same time, however, political scientists' findings may have been influenced by the fact that their studies investigated the relationship between PAC contributions and roll call votes, which may not be where political contributions have their greatest impact. Money may be more likely to influence the content of legislation than the votes of individual members on bills. Since the late 1970s, Congress has increasingly voted on large bills that fold together spending on many areas. These votes frequently take place with little debate—in some cases before the bill has even been printed for members of Congress to read. Because their passage is often a foregone conclusion, what ends up in these bills is quite important. Interest groups therefore have a strong incentive to affect the content of such legislation.

Thus, in 1996, when GOP leaders dropped into legislation language that would have given the tobacco industry a major financial advantage, the relationship between money and policy would not have shown up as PAC contributions affecting roll call votes: first, few legislators apparently knew about the provision when the vote was taken; second, the money that may have influenced GOP leaders to include the provision would have been large donations of soft money from tobacco companies.

Over the past several years, the media have brought to light a number of cases in which specific favors for major donors were embedded in obscure language in legislation. It seems likely that the provisions were the direct result of political contributions. It is worth noting that in most cases, once the media have made an issue of these favors, Congress has repealed them. Political contributions are thus less influential than public outcry, but are nonetheless probably important in influencing the content of some legislation.

Thus, it may well be that PAC money does not buy roll call votes but does have an important influence on the content of legislation. Two unrelated trends may account for this situation: First, legislation is more and more likely to be worked out by party leaders in closed-door sessions (Sinclair 1997). This pattern is particularly characteristic of the new Republican Congress, where party leaders have put considerable pressure on committees and even bypassed them on important occasions. Although this approach has enabled the House to move quickly to pass important legislation, it has also made it easier for party leaders to insert language into bills without having it subject to the committees' deliberative processes. Second, the sharp increase in party efforts to raise soft money provides interest groups with the opportunity to give far more than they could give through PACs. Taken together, these trends mean that the temptation for party leaders to insert special provisions to reward the party's largest donors is likely to increase.

Regardless of whether money actually buys public policy, the public overwhelmingly believes that wealthy interests receive favors for their political contributions, and this belief exacerbates the growing cynicism about the American political system. One survey found that a substantial majority of Americans were worried that political contributions had too much influence on public policy, and nearly half believed that campaign contributions sometimes lead elected officials to support policies that they do not believe are in the best interests of the country (Center for Responsive Politics 1998). The survey also revealed that one aspect of campaign finance that respondents found particularly troubling is the fact that policy makers schedule fund raising events at the same time that they are considering policy that affects interest groups.

Although political parties and incumbents have long used their power over the policy agenda to extract resources from interest groups, such activity appears to have increased in recent years. During the visibly frantic fund raising undertaken during the 1996 campaign, both Republicans and Democrats were increasingly likely to design and schedule fund-raising events so that interest groups were being asked for contributions immediately before scheduled deliberations on legislation that would affect them. Such unseemly conduct signals the need for comprehensive campaign finance reform, which we will discuss later in the chapter.

Interest Groups and Voters

With the American electorate often poorly informed about the political positions of the members of the House and Senate who represent them—and even about the positions of major presidential candidates—communication between interest groups and voters is often vital to the democratic process. Endorsements, "hit lists," and voters' guides provide citizens with information they need and enable them to "vote their interests." Voters for whom abortion is a salient issue, for example, can easily find a voters' guide from a pro-choice or anti-abortion group to guide their choices at the ballot box. In an era of weak political parties and candidate-centered, media-driven campaigns, interest groups play a crucial role by assessing the candidates' records, not just their rhetoric.

Often, however, voters' guides provide misleading and even false information. Moreover, they are more and more likely to be published by tax-exempt organizations claiming to be nonpartisan; given the content of the guides, such claims make a mockery of tax and campaign finance laws. And when interest groups receive money from political parties to conduct "nonpartisan" voter mobilization efforts, it is clear that everyone involved is doing their utmost to evade the law.

Because issue advocacy campaigns were waged for the first time in 1996, it is difficult to determine their ultimate impact on American elections. On the one hand, organized and coordinated efforts to inform the voters of candidates' positions and records can serve a valuable educational function. Moreover, to seek to persuade voters to adopt a particular position on the issues of the day is a clear exercise of the constitutional right to freedom of speech.

Nevertheless, issue advocacy campaigns seem to raise some thorny problems. First, they have the effect of shifting policy debate from candidates to loose coalitions of interest groups. Although political scientists disagree strongly about whether policy messages should be shaped by the parties or by the candidates, few would argue that interest groups should dominate this process. When interest groups frame the issues, attack the character of candidates, and otherwise run shadow campaigns, accountability suffers. Candidates are not responsible for the claims and attacks in the advertisements, and it is more difficult to hold candidates to campaign promises when those promises are made by interest groups and not by the candidates themselves.

Second, in 1996, issue advocacy campaigns were funded in several states by special, ad-hoc organizations apparently assembled for the explicit purpose of attacking or defending particular candidates. Bearing names such as "Citizens for Reform" and "Citizens for Republican Education Fund," such organizations are unknown entities to the voters. If they survive and grow, then candidates, parties, and interest groups will come to know them and the figures behind them; but it may be that each election cycle will spawn a new set of shadow groups that persist for only that cycle and then dissolve. Such a development would be highly undesirable, for it would mean that significant spending in the late weeks of elections would come from unknown sources with unknown agendas.

Third, issue advocacy campaigns are often a way to skirt campaign finance laws. Technically, the purpose of these campaigns is to advocate issues, not the election of candidates, but many interest groups that undertook such campaigns in 1996 publicly admitted that they sought to influence elections. Issue advocacy is thus a means of spending unlimited amounts to help or hurt individual candidates.

Fourth, and perhaps most important, because issue advocacy can be conducted without revealing either expenditures or donors, it undermines the disclosure system, the most successful aspect of the current campaign finance regime. In order to determine whether a candidate appears to have been unduly influenced by "special interests," it is vital for the media, the parties, citizens, and interest groups to be able to discover where contributions have come from and how extensive they are. When interest groups can spend unlimited amounts of undisclosed and untraceable funds, the disclosure system is perhaps fatally damaged—which is, in turn, likely to increase public cynicism about the political system.

REFORMING THE SYSTEM

Every aspect of interest group involvement in campaigns has its critics, who often differ widely on proposals for reform. In this section of the chapter, we will discuss the major types of proposed reforms and identify those that we believe would improve the electoral process. Before looking at specific proposed reforms, we need to emphasize that reform is never "complete": each set of reforms becomes part of an ongoing process intended to correct the defects of the system.

One danger of campaign reform is that it sometimes has unexpected consequences. In 1971, when Congress was drafting the Federal Election Campaign Act (FECA), the AFL-CIO pushed for the inclusion of language to legalize political action committees (PACs) so that the labor-sponsored Committee on Political Education (COPE) could continue to exist. Labor strategists did not expect corporations (and, later, ideological groups) to form PACs—which they did, at a rapid rate, in the late 1970s and early 1980s. Nor did those members of Congress who drafted the language for the FECA anticipate that during most of the 1980s and 1990s, PACs would contribute half of the money raised by House incumbents. Similarly, in 1979, when Congress allowed soft money to be raised to help build the parties, it did not anticipate that by 1996, soft money would be used to help elect federal candidates and would constitute a significant portion of all money raised in federal campaigns.

Because reforms have unintended consequences and because interest groups and political parties hire lawyers and political experts to help them identify and exploit loopholes in the law, reform must be an ongoing process. Congress has regulated the relationship between interest groups and elections in fits of sporadic reform, whenever scandals have sparked public demand for action. The last major campaign finance legislation was passed in 1974 and amended in 1979. During the two decades that fol-lowed, further tinkering with the law could have helped close loopholes; but by 1998, many of these loopholes had become part of the established procedures for conducting campaigns.

Interest Groups and Parties

The role that interest groups play in the nomination process is central to their relationship with political parties. Scholars have proposed a variety of reforms for the nomination process, the most common of which would give party leaders greater control—in some cases complete control—over nominations. Such proposals are not new: in the 1970s and early 1980s, for example, many political scientists argued that the system for nominating presidential candidates should return more control to party elites. In the Democratic Party, the creation of "superdelegates," who are primarily elected officials, was in part a response to such suggestions; the decision to compress the schedule of primaries and caucuses was also intended to pro-vide greater influence for party moderates and to give an advantage to well-known "insider" candidates. Similarly, the GOP has retained its "win-ner-take-all" system of selecting delegates, in part to prevent ideological candidates with limited appeal from sending large delegations to the national convention. Although it is clear that party nomination rules do affect who wins (Lengle and Shafer 1976), it is not clear that such rules consistently help or hurt different types of candidates—largely because campaign professionals are constantly looking for new ways to help their candidates win under different sets of rules.

Another proposed reform would create a single national primary elec-tion or four regional primary elections. The goal would be to weaken the impact of Iowa and New Hampshire on the nomination process; both are states in which interest groups are strongly represented. The current system forces candidates to run for several weeks in many states, appealing to groups that are perhaps disproportionately important in each state. In 1988, for example, Michael Dukakis announced his support for the American Civil Liberties Union (ACLU), in part to appeal to party activists and members of liberal interest groups in Iowa. The move came back to haunt him in the general election, when George Bush attacked the ACLU for defending some unsavory and unpopular causes. Proponents of national or regional primaries argue that they will lead to the election of more cen-trist candidates who are established national politicians and that they will help candidates resist making promises to interest groups that are especially influential in states that are crucial to the election calendar.

Yet such reforms could well have unexpected consequences, as occurred in 1988 with the creation of Super Tuesday, a multistate primary day centered in the South. Super Tuesday was an effort by southern Democrats to reassert their influence on the party—which, they hoped, would pull the party to the center—but Jesse Jackson and Michael Dukakis were the big winners in the South (Norrander 1992). It is difficult to anticipate the precise effects of national or regional primaries, but they would likely favor candidates who could raise money quickly—either sitting governors of large states or members of Congress with control over the policy agenda, who could attract funding from economic groups such as corporations or labor unions; or ideological candidates with well-honed direct-mail fundraising lists. (See Brown, Powell, and Wilcox 1995 for a discussion of presidential fund raising.) Moreover, it is not immediately clear that a national or regional primary system would decrease the power of grassroots ideological groups. Interest groups that could mobilize a large membership to support endorsed candidates would continue to play an important role in nomination politics, and candidates would still need to appeal to such groups for their votes. Moreover, without the winnowing process that currently exists, even ideologically extreme candidates might fare quite well: in a single, crowded national primary field, it would not be difficult for an ideological candidate with narrow factional appeal to win with a relatively small plurality of the votes.

Although there has been less discussion of changes in the nomination process for congressional candidates, allowing party leaders to choose the nominees for these races would have a profound impact on the relationship between parties and interest groups. Consider, for example, a 1998 GOP primary for a special election in California to replace a Democratic incumbent who had died. House Speaker Newt Gingrich, R-Ga., openly backed moderate assemblyman Brooks Firestone for the seat, but antiabortion groups ran an issue advocacy campaign on behalf of Assemblyman Tom Bordonaro that attacked Firestone for supporting late-term abortions. Bordonaro pledged that if elected to the House he would not support Gingrich as Speaker, thereby ensuring increased divisions in the House GOP. Bordonaro won the primary but lost the general election to the incumbent's widow. If Gingrich or the Republican Congressional Campaign Committee (RCCC) had been able to select Firestone for the seat and Firestone had won the general election, he would have owed his election to the party leaders. If they later asked for his vote on important legislation, he would have been forced to comply; if he refused, the party would have the option of selecting a different candidate to run in the next election. Allowing party leaders to choose nominees for congressional office would increase party discipline and greatly simplify the tasks facing voters. If all members supported and opposed the same policies, voters would merely have to determine what each party—rather than each candidate—stood for.

Such a change would not mean, of course, that interest groups would cease to play any role in party nominations. Anti-abortion forces are active in the RCCC, and there is a strong anti-abortion contingent in the House GOP: these groups would pressure Gingrich, or whoever made the decision, to support candidates who took the anti-abortion pledge. Groups with significant resources—including ardent followers who contribute money to campaigns, vote loyally for party candidates, and volunteer to distribute voters' guides—would still be in a position to insist that some candidates share their policy preferences and probably also that some candidates come from the activist ranks of the group itself. But party leaders would bargain with interest groups centrally and could determine, to a certain extent, the ideological composition of their congressional delegation.

Of course, if American parties became disciplined, unified organizations like European parties, then interest groups would have even more at stake in battles over party platforms. Indeed, it is quite possible that if any platform document bound all members of the party to support a particular policy on abortion, the GOP itself would fragment and divide.

It seems unlikely that members of the major political parties or members of Congress would permit the parties to adopt rules that would deny them access to the nomination ballot. America's decentralized federal system poses another obstacle to centralized party control of nominations: state parties are heavily regulated by state law, and some states require that political parties hold primary elections to nominate their candidates. Moreover, it is unlikely that party officials in Texas, for example, would support a proposal to let party leaders in Washington, D.C., select their state party candidates. State laws can change, and it might be possible for increasing numbers of states to allow state party leaders to choose the candidates directly, but this change might simply shift the focus of conflict from party primaries to the election of party chairs and committees.

Term limits are yet another proposed reform that would affect the relationship between parties and interest groups. If incumbents were prohibited from serving more than a small number of terms, politicians would have to plan for life after Capitol Hill. Term limits might, for example, encourage corporate executives to run for office, with their companies guaranteeing them jobs when their terms end. Term limits might also increase the influence of ideological groups on the nomination process: with a field devoid of professional politicians, the intensity of group support could easily swing primary election outcomes. Finally, once in office, many incumbents would seek to establish ties with interest groups that might hire them when their terms are up.

Of course, parties are free to tinker with the rules that affect nominations, delegate selection, and the writing of platforms. If the Democratic Party chose to, it could adopt a winner-take-all system of delegate selection, although many important party constituencies would react with outrage. It could include many more superdelegates at the convention, or it could allow all delegates to be free agents regardless of the outcome of primary elections in their states. The GOP could change the way its delegates are selected, requiring that delegates come from the lists provided by the candidates; it could also change the way the party platform is drafted to give the nominee much more say in the language. Such changes would affect the balance of power between contending interests in the parties for a time, although the long-term consequences are unpredictable.

Interest Groups, Candidates, and Voters

Controversy over the relationship between interest groups and candidates and interest groups and voters is almost exclusively focused on campaign finance. By 1996, there was near consensus among political scientists, policy analysts, and many politicians that the campaign finance system was badly in need of reform. Addressing the Senate in support of the bill he cosponsored with GOP senator John McCain, Ariz., Democratic senator Russell Feingold, Wis., observed, "I think it is clear, Mr. President, that the few remaining pillars holding up our crumbling election system finally collapsed." In the preface to the package of campaign finance proposals created by the Brookings Institution Working Group, political scientists Norman J. Ornstein, Thomas E. Mann, Paul Taylor, Michael J. Malbin, and Anthony Corrado Jr. noted that

> the campaign finance system in America . . . in 1996 . . . went from the political equivalent of a low-grade fever to Code Blue—from a chronic

problem needing attention sooner or later to a crisis, with a system clearly out of control" (Ornstein et al. 1997).

Similarly, a task force on campaign finance assembled by Herbert Alexander, of the Citizens' Research Foundation, argued that by allowing unlimited amounts of money to flow outside of the disclosure system, changes in campaign financing have created problems of accountability (Alexander et al. 1997).

The reason that so many academics, political consultants, and even politicians sound so alarmed is that the system of campaign finance changed dramatically in the 1996 elections, and the changes appear to portend a radical shift from a regime in which PACs and individuals finance campaigns to one in which interest group treasuries provide most of the money in elections. As noted in Chapter 1, between 1974 and 1996, individuals were the main source of funding for presidential and congressional campaigns, while PACs played an important role in House elections. PACs raised their money through regulated contributions from individual members and contributed most of that money in regulated contributions to candidates.

As shown in Figure 5-1, a record amount of soft money flooded into the system in the 1996 elections. Soft money contributions are disclosed to the Federal Election Commission (FEC) but are not limited in size; moreover, interest groups can draw on treasury funds—from union dues or corporate profits, for example—to make soft money contributions.

In addition, interest groups spent at least $135 million on issue advocacy campaigns in 1996 (although the total amount will never be known), along with countless millions on "nonpartisan" voters' guides—all from their treasuries, and all undisclosed to the public.

Many observers are concerned that future campaigns will be conducted by shifting alliances of interest groups—some of which, backed by unknown funding sources and designed to further unknown agendas, will be created solely to spend money in a particular campaign. Moreover, when significant portions of campaign funds are drawn from interest group treasuries, there is a potential for tremendous imbalances, as wealthier groups can easily outspend those with fewer financial resources. Although we do not believe that too much money is spent on elections or that money is the only resource that matters in elections, we nonetheless feel that the time has come for serious reform.

A staggering range of more than seventy campaign finance proposals was put before the 105th Congress. Some recommended public financing,

FIGURE 5-1
Soft Money Fund Raising in Presidential Election Cycles

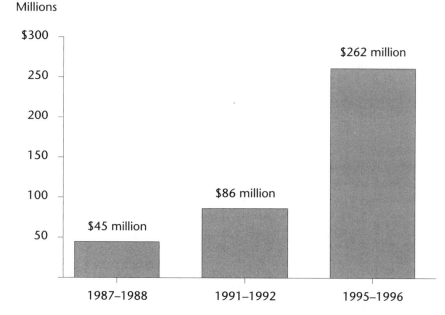

Millions

$300

$262 million

250

200

150

100        $86 million

$45 million

50

1987–1988   1991–1992   1995–1996

Source: Home page, Common Cause. http://www.commoncause.org/publications/ return_1.htm.

while others would unleash parties to collect and spend private money; some would impose strict spending limits, while at least one would have abolished all limits; some encouraged small individual donations, others gifts from within the district; still others increased the limit on all individual gifts.

At one extreme are proposals that would essentially lift all spending restrictions, requiring disclosure only of the source of the money and how it is spent. There are two principal arguments advanced for such plans: first, spending and contributing are forms of free speech, which should not be limited; second, because those with money to give will always find loopholes in regulatory systems, restrictions on contributions and spending have failed. Those who make the second argument often compare money to a raging torrent that will inevitably find a way over, around, or through a dam.

The elimination of all spending limits has attracted little support except among libertarian groups and Republican politicians. Critics charge that it would allow the wealthiest groups to dominate elections and dramatically increase both the perception and reality of political corruption.

At the other extreme are proposals that would eliminate private money from elections altogether, substituting public funds. Many Western European democracies currently have systems in which the government provides money to the parties to spend on behalf of their candidates; and, as we saw in Chapter 2, public financing exists in a limited form at the presidential level in the United States. Proponents of public financing argue that it would actually save money: first, by eliminating the need for legislators to provide interest groups with particularistic economic benefits such as tax cuts and corporate welfare; and second, by eliminating not only most corruption but the appearance of it as well. Candidates who accepted public funding would agree to refuse private money and to limit their spending to the public grant, a policy which the Supreme Court has already upheld.

Although it has worked well in other democracies, it is difficult to know how public funding might work in the United States. Independent expenditures and issue advocacy would still be permitted, although there may be ways to make them less attractive to interest groups. Critics charge that public funding would create yet another entitlement program, this time for politicians. Moreover, they argue that the system would be costly and would give public money to candidates who might espouse unpalatable and even offensive views. A more limited form of public funding—perhaps providing a small amount to all general election or even primary election candidates to help them launch their campaigns—would be less expensive and would foster electoral competition. Moreover, if candidates accepted these funds they could be bound to abide by other limits in the law.

Many reform proposals include spending limits for candidates, which the Supreme Court has ruled enforceable only for those who accept some form of public subsidy. Under such proposals, candidates would agree to spend only a certain amount, perhaps $500,000 in House races, with a variable amount—depending on the size of the state—for the Senate. The case for spending limits is that by preventing incumbents from simply drowning out their opponents' messages with a constant barrage of advertisements, they create a more level playing field and foster genuine competition. The case against such limits is that limits set too low would protect incumbents (because challengers must spend large sums to achieve the name recognition necessary to compete), and limits set too high would serve little purpose at all. Moreover, spending by candidates is clearly political speech in its most pure form, and any limits on it must be approached with caution.

Some proposals would ban or severely limit PACs. Proponents argue that this would reduce the power of special interests in financing elections. Yet a ban or sharp limits on PACs seem likely to produce exactly the opposite effect: with access to PACs restricted or denied, interest groups would channel their money into issue advocacy, and individual members would contribute directly to candidates instead of to the PAC. Both tactics would render it much more difficult to assess the total amount contributed or spent by an interest group; although it is easy to determine, for example, that a PAC is sponsored by a particular corporation, it is much harder to discover which individuals are associated with that corporation.

Supporters of a related proposal, to eliminate or severely limit soft money, argue that soft money is the major source of scandal and potential corruption in the current system and that banning it would force interest groups to give through their PACs, using money raised from their members. Critics of this proposal argue that soft money is necessary for political parties to develop and articulate their messages.

Other proposals would ban bundling of individual donations. Supporters charge that bundling allows interest groups to avoid limits on contributions and that banning such gifts would level the playing field. But because bundling is one way for interest groups with limited funds but many dedicated members to marshal their resources for a campaign, banning such activity would simply increase the advantage that traditional economic interests—such as corporations and labor unions—already have in elections. Moreover, any ban on bundling would almost certainly be struck down by the Supreme Court; but even if it were not, it would be quite simple to evade. EMILY's List now collects envelopes and passes them to the candidate, but if bundling were banned, the group could simply invite its members to give to Sen. Barbara Boxer, D-Calif., and provide them with special EMILY's List envelopes in which to do so. Corporations would simply sponsor tables at fund-raising events, as they often do today.

Still other proposals would limit Senate and House candidates to raising money within their state or district or would require that a certain percentage—perhaps a majority—of their receipts come from their state or district. Supporters and critics of such reforms tend to have differing views of representation. Supporters tend to think of representation as geographic; in their view, members of Congress represent voters in their states or districts, who should therefore fund their campaigns. Critics tend to think of representation as ideological or demographic; they argue that the views of many Americans are not necessarily represented by the legislators elected to represent their state or district but may be represented by other national leaders.

Finally, in 1998, Republicans and business interests began a push to ban unions from spending treasury funds on political causes. Polls showed that voters favored such changes, although it was clear that many did not fully understand their implications: namely, that corporations would still be free to spend millions on issue advocacy and to give millions in soft money, whereas labor unions would be powerless to redress the imbalance. In California, Republicans unsuccessfully pushed for a ballot initiative that would ban unions from spending treasury funds in elections in that state.

Because the parties cannot even agree on the definitions of problems let alone the desirability of proposed solutions, by mid-1998 serious campaign finance reform has evaded Congress. House Republicans, once the champions of radical reform, profit from the current system. Democrats—desperate to recapture control of Congress before the GOP majority firmly entrenches itself—decry soft money, but they have become increasingly dependent on it to counter the growing Republican advantage in PAC contributions.

Although teams of political scientists have proposed significant reforms, no clear consensus about either the nature of the problems or the solutions has emerged. The task force assembled by Herbert Alexander issued a thoughtful and provocative report and set of recommendations, but the nine scholars generated three separate dissents on topics such as spending limits, limits on party contributions, and constitutional issues (Alexander et al. 1997). And despite some overlap in membership, the Alexander task force and the Brookings Institution Working Group suggested different reforms (Ornstein et al. 1997).

The reform proposals circulating through academia, foundations, government watchdog groups, and Congress are so broad and numerous that we cannot review them all here. Instead, we will highlight some of the most interesting and diverse elements of various proposals, then indicate the elements of reform that we personally favor. It is likely, moreover, that whatever reforms are finally enacted will differ from those currently under consideration, as the process of congressional deliberation proceeds through bargaining and compromise.

DIRECTIONS FOR CAMPAIGN FINANCE REFORM

Although we support different political parties and disagree on a number of political issues, we do agree on a set of general principles that should guide reformers and on many specific reforms as well.

Underlying Assumptions

Our sense of where campaign finance reform needs to be directed is based on a number of assumptions. First, we wish to protect interest group activities that help group members develop political abilities and that educate and inform voters about issues and candidates' positions. By training their members and educating them in the workings of the political process, interest groups help democratize the political system, ensuring that political expertise is not confined solely to the wealthiest and best-educated citizens. Because we also value the diversity of voices in the political system and the inclusion of previously disenfranchised groups, we favor reforms that promote grassroots activity and that encourage individual members of interest groups to participate in elections by volunteering time and money.

Second, we greatly value the freedoms of speech and association that interest groups claim as the basis for many of their activities. Nevertheless, we do not equate limits on spending with limits on speech. Campaign spending drives up the costs of advertising, which puts less wealthy groups at a disadvantage in getting their message out. Because voters have a limited attention span when it comes to politics, they tend to focus on the most frequent and familiar themes. Although there will always be disparities among interest groups in the ability to compete in and influence elections, we favor reforms that help level the playing field, enabling diverse interest groups to make their positions public. When the wealthiest interest groups can spend unlimited amounts to advocate their positions, political debate and deliberation are perhaps least inclusive, and many important voices are likely to go unheard.

Third, we value electoral competition and therefore generally support activities that allow nonincumbent candidates to achieve the name recognition and media attention needed to communicate their views. Our views on this issue are not based on the assumption that incumbents win elections only by outspending their opponents: most incumbents are experienced candidates who have survived many elections because they have strong political skills and are a good fit in their state or district. Instead, we believe that challengers deserve the right to state their case in an election, and to do so they must be able to raise and spend sufficient sums.

Fourth, we value a fully transparent system of disclosure of campaign activities. Although too comprehensive and rigid a disclosure system could have a chilling effect on small and local interest groups, it is also true that operating in secret creates opportunities for corruption. Perhaps more important, voters are much more likely to perceive the system as corrupt when they cannot discover precisely how interest groups have aided political candidates. We therefore believe that political activities conducted without disclosure of the amounts spent and the sources of the revenue are potentially damaging to democracy.

Finally, we prefer that interest groups' campaign activities strengthen the candidates' and parties' accountability to citizens. Thus, we support proposals that would encourage interest groups to channel money to candidates and parties and that would discourage them from engaging in issue advocacy and independent expenditures. Stronger political parties and campaigns in which the candidates articulate the issues are preferable to campaigns driven by interest groups.

Goals of Reform

Generally, we support reforms that would channel money through candidates, parties, and PACs; that would limit the size of contributions; and that would push more financial activity into the disclosure system. Moreover, we support proposals that would increase the competitiveness of campaigns, fostering a flow of resources to nonincumbents in the crucial early stages of their campaigns. Many contending proposals claim to achieve these goals, but continued dialogue and study will be needed to uncover the implications of these plans; in addition, whatever individual reforms are adopted must be part of an ongoing process that modifies the rules as fund-raising technologies and practices change.

To create more competitive campaigns, some analysts have proposed partial public funding for general election candidates (as now exists in the presidential nomination process). Others prefer free or subsidized media time for candidates, and still others have proposed increasing the limit on the initial amount of money raised by candidates so that they can more expeditiously launch their campaigns. Such proposals could be expanded to include candidates in primary elections as well. We are especially drawn to the idea of free or subsidized media. The Brookings Institution Working Group, for example, calls for a "broadcast bank" of minutes of television and radio time to be distributed to major party candidates and to major and minor political parties.

A system of partial matching funds—perhaps matching the first $10,000 in individual contributions of $500 or less raised by a candidate—would also enable candidates to more effectively launch their campaigns, thereby helping to make elections more competitive. It would have the additional benefit of creating an incentive to raise small contributions. Tax credits for small individual contributions are worth exploring, although we are not certain that they would provide a strong incentive to give.

We would ban soft money contributions but would make it easier for parties to raise hard money from individuals and PACs by raising the limits on individual and PAC contributions to parties. By increasing the limits on hard money contributions to parties and candidates, we hope to encourage interest groups to make direct contributions rather than to undertake issue advocacy campaigns. Moreover, we would weaken current limits on the ability of parties to channel their money into the most competitive elections.

It is unclear at this time what kinds of limitations on issue advocacy might pass muster with the Supreme Court. Moreover, we do not think that all issue advocacy should be banned: activity that is genuinely intended to promote an issue rather than a candidate is clearly protected free speech. We would, however, favor several requirements: first, that corporations, labor unions, trade associations, and membership groups be required to pay for issue advocacy through voluntary funds raised from group members or other sympathetic individuals; second, that these funds be maintained as segregated funds—in other words, through PACs. Contributions to these segregated funds should be limited, and all contributions and spending should be disclosed to the FEC.

Moreover, any communication that uses the name or image of a candidate close to the date of a primary or general election campaign should be defined as an electoral activity. Thus, such communication would be conducted through the existing regulatory framework—that is, through PAC money raised from individual group members and from other committees. Such a system would not limit the ability of interest groups to spend on behalf of candidates (they could still make unlimited independent expenditures), but it would channel the money through the current disclosure system and subject it to individual contribution limits. We oppose any limits on the use of union treasury funds in electoral activity unless they are balanced by a ban on similar corporate activities.

We think that incentives should be structured (1) to encourage interest groups to concentrate on raising money from individuals and contributing it to candidates and parties and (2) to engage less in issue advocacy and independent expenditure campaigns. The development of incentives will likely be an ongoing process, but one way to begin might be to allow candidates who are attacked by major issue advocacy or independent expenditure campaigns to have additional time from the broadcast bank to answer such advertising. Another option is to require that stations that accept issue advocacy ads in the period before an election allow candidates to purchase rebuttal time at a steep discount.

Finally, we favor strengthening the enforcement powers of the FEC to make it easier to draft new regulations to deal with the changing realities of campaign finance. Because individuals and organizations will always seek ways to avoid limits imposed by the law, reform must be an ongoing process.

Taken together, the reforms we support would not place undue limits on the ability of interest groups to play an active role in campaigns. Instead, the reforms would accomplish three goals: first, encourage interest groups to undertake activities that are disclosed; second, encourage them to undertake activities that are funded by voluntary contributions from individual group members; third, channel money to candidates and parties— in other words, to entities that can be held responsible for the content of communications. Compelling interest groups to rely more heavily on voluntary contributions would likely strengthen them: to raise the money necessary to participate fully in elections, interest groups would have to develop more actively politicized members.

It should be noted, however, that money does not ensure election; indeed, many well-funded candidates have lost to candidates with less money but broader public support. Helping challengers raise money will help make elections more competitive, but reforming the redistricting process would go much further toward that end. Allowing state legislators and governors to draw district boundaries has created many districts in which one party is assured of victory. Moreover, the boundaries often make little political or cultural sense, except as vehicles to protect incumbents or to maximize the number of seats that can be won by one party or the other. A more fair, less partisan way to draw district lines might go further toward increasing competition in elections than campaign finance reform.

SUMMARY

Interest groups are, and always have been, controversial yet necessary players in the American electoral process. According to their critics, interest groups distort the political process in favor of the better organized and better funded, subverting true democracy. In the eyes of their defenders, interest groups are a bulwark of our democracy, embodying the Madisonian notion of a competitive pluralist system.

Although we were dismayed by many campaign practices of various interest groups in the 1996 elections, we believe that interest groups are essential to American democracy. Reform is perhaps more needed today than ever before: without reform, it is clear that interest groups will come to dominate the messages of campaigns, drowning out the voices of candidates and parties alike.

Despite the evident need for reform, entrenched interests appear to be protecting the current system, and we are discouraged about the prospects for genuine change. It is especially discouraging that in the late 1990s, despite public clamor for reform, Congress could not even agree on whether reform is needed, let alone which reforms to enact.

Ironically, the difficulty of changing the role of interest groups in elections is a reflection of the pluralist system itself. As Madison predicted, a pluralist system requires compromise to be forged among diverse interests with different views; policy change in America thus comes about slowly, after much debate and deliberation. As we have seen, even among those who agree that reform is necessary, there is little agreement on what exactly should be done.

List of References

Adams, Greg D. 1996. "Times of tumult: Abortion and the transformation of American political parties." Ph.D. diss., University of Iowa.

Alexander, Herbert J., et al. 1997. *New realities, new thinking.* Citizens' Research Foundation. http://www.usc.edu/dept/CRF/DATA/newrnewt.htm.

Appleton, Andrew, and Daniel Francis. 1997. "Washington: Mobilizing for victory." In *God at the grass roots, 1996: The Christian right in American elections,* ed. Mark J. Rozell and Clyde Wilcox. Lanham, Md.: Rowman & Littlefield.

Babcock, Charles, and Richard Morin. 1988. "Bush's money machine." *Washington Post,* 15 May.

Baer, Denise L., and David A. Bositis. 1993. *Elite cadres and party coalitions.* New York: Greenwood Press.

Baida, Peter. 1992. "The legacy of Dollar Mark Hanna." In *The quest for national office,* ed. Stephen J. Wayne and Clyde Wilcox. New York: St. Martin's.

Banfield, Edward C. 1980. "In defense of the party system." In *Political parties in the eighties,* ed. Robert A. Goldwin. Washington, D.C.: American Enterprise Institute.

Beck, Deborah, et al. 1997. *Issue advocacy advertising during the 1996 campaign.* Philadelphia: Annenberg Public Policy Center.

Bedlington, Anne. 1994. "The National Association of Realtors PAC: Rules or rationality?" In *Risky business: PAC decisionmaking in congressional elections,* ed. Robert Biersack, Paul S. Herrnson, and Clyde Wilcox. Armonk, N.Y.: M. E. Sharpe.

___. Forthcoming. "The Realtors, Political Action Committee: Covering All Contingencies." In *After the revolution: PACs and lobbies in the new Republican Congress,* ed. Robert Biersack, Paul Herrnson, and Clyde Wilcox. New York: Allyn and Bacon.

Bennet, James. 1996a. "With GOP convention, ad campaigns gear up." *New York Times,* 7 August.

___. 1996b. "Most delegates conservative, male, and white." *New York Times,* 12 August.

Biersack, Robert, Paul S. Herrnson, and Clyde Wilcox, eds. 1993. "Seeds for success: Early money in congressional elections." *Legislative Studies Quarterly* 18: 535–552.

___. 1994. *Risky business: PAC decisionmaking in congressional elections.* Armonk, N.Y.: M. E. Sharpe.

BIPAC (Business-Industry Political Action Committee). 1996. *Rising to the challenge in 1996: What business groups must do to protect free enterprise majorities in Congress.* Washington, D.C.: BIPAC.

Broder, David. 1972. *The party's over.* New York: Harper and Row.

Brown, Clifford, Lynda Powell, and Clyde Wilcox. 1995. *Serious money: Fundraising and contributing in presidential nomination campaigns.* New York: Cambridge University Press.

Bruce, John. 1997. "Texas: A success story, at least for now." In *God at the grass roots, 1996: The Christian right in American elections,* ed. Mark J. Rozell and Clyde Wilcox. Lanham, Md.: Rowman & Littlefield.

Bruce, John, and Clyde Wilcox. 1998. "Introduction." In *The changing politics of gun control,* ed. John Bruce and Clyde Wilcox. Lanham, Md.: Rowman & Littlefield.

Bullock, Charles S., III, and John Christopher Grant. 1995. "Georgia: The Christian right and grass roots power." In *God at the grass roots, 1994: The Christian right in American elections,* ed. Mark J. Rozell and Clyde Wilcox. Lanham, Md.: Rowman & Littlefield.

Bullock, Charles S., III, and Mark C. Smith. 1997. "Georgia: Purists, pragmatists, and electoral outcomes." In *God at the grass roots, 1996: The Christian right in American elections,* ed. Mark J. Rozell and Clyde Wilcox. Lanham, Md.: Rowman & Littlefield.

Cannon, Lou. 1998. "California house race leaves.'passionate centrist' behind." *Washington Post,* 15 January.

Cantor, David. Forthcoming. "The Sierra Club Political Committee." In *After the revolution: PACs and lobbies in the new Republican Congress,* ed. Robert Biersack, Paul S. Herrnson, and Clyde Wilcox. New York: Allyn and Bacon.

Caro, Robert. 1982. *The years of Lyndon Johnson: The path to power.* New York: Knopf.

Ceaser, James. 1979. *Presidential selection.* Princeton, N.J.: Princeton University Press.

——. 1982. *Reforming the reforms.* Cambridge, Mass.: Ballinger.

Center for Responsive Politics. 1998. Washington, D.C. Survey conducted by Princeton Research Associates. http://www.crp.org/index.htm.

Chapell, Henry W. 1982. "Campaign contributions and congressional voting: A simultaneous probit-tobit model." *Review of Economics and Statistics* 62: 77–83.

"Christians rally for pro-life at outdoor meeting." 1996. CNN. Transcript. AllPolitics. com/CNN. 14 August.

Cigler, Allan J., and Burdett A. Loomis. 1997. "Kansas: The Christian right and the new mainstream of Republican politics." In *God at the grass roots, 1996: The Christian right in American elections,* ed. Mark J. Rozell and Clyde Wilcox. Lanham, Md.: Rowman & Littlefield.

Cleland, Sen. Max. 1997. Presentation to the Washington Semester Seminar at The American University, Washington, D.C., 29 October.

Clines, Francis X. 1996. "San Diego diary: Bored with the big tent? Then go to the sideshow." *New York Times,* 16 August.

"Clinton assails Dole on tobacco and liquor company on TV ads." 1996. *New York Times,* 16 June.

Clymer, Adam. 1997. "Organized labor goes on the offensive, and the Republicans cry foul." *New York Times,* 20 July.

Common Cause. 1998. *Return on investment: The hidden story of soft money, corporate welfare, and the 1997 budget and tax deal.* Washington, D.C.: Common Cause.

Cook, Elizabeth Adell, Ted Jelen, and Clyde Wilcox. 1992. *Between two absolutes: Public opinion and the politics of abortion.* Boulder, Colo.: Western.

Corrado, Anthony, Jr. 1992. *Creative campaigning: PACs and the presidential selection.* Boulder, Colo.: Westview.

Drew, Elizabeth. 1997. *Whatever it takes: The real struggle for political power in America.* New York: Viking.

Duerst-Lahti, Georgia. 1998. "Introduction: Women and elective office." In *Women and elective office,* ed. Sue Thomas and Clyde Wilcox. New York: Cambridge University Press.

Edsall, Thomas. 1995. "Robertson urges Christian activists to take over GOP." *Washington Post,* 10 September.

Eismeier, Theodore J., and Philip H. Pollock III. 1984. "Political action committees: Varieties of organization and strategy." In *Money and politics in the United States,* ed. Michael Malbin. Chatham, N.J.: Chatham House.

——. 1985. "An organizational analysis of political action committees." *Political Behavior* 7: 192–216.

Epstein, Edwin. 1980. "Business and labor under the Federal Election Campaign Act of 1971." In *Parties, interest groups, and campaign finance laws,* ed. Michael Malbin. Washington, D.C.: American Enterprise Institute.

Ferrara, Joseph. 1994. "The Eaton Corporation Public Policy Association: Ideology, pragmatism, and big business." In *Risky business: PAC decisionmaking in congressional elections,* ed. Robert Biersack, Paul S. Herrnson, and Clyde Wilcox. Armonk, N.Y.: M. E. Sharpe.

Fisher, William L., Ralph Reed Jr., and Richard L. Weinhold. 1990. *Christian Coalition leadership manual.* Chesapeake, Va.: Christian Coalition.

Fowler, Linda L., and Robert D. McClure. 1989. *Political ambition: Who decides to run for Congress?* New Haven: Yale University Press.

Gallup Poll. 1984. *The presidential election: Exit poll.* 7 November. Princeton, N.J.: Gallup.

Gerber, Robin. Forthcoming. "Building to win, building to last: The AFL-CIO COPE takes on the Republican Congress." In *After the revolution: PACs and lobbies in the new Repub-*

lican Congress, ed. Robert Biersack, Paul S. Herrnson, and Clyde Wilcox. New York: Allyn and Bacon.

Gilbert, Christopher P., and David A. Peterson. 1995. "Minnesota: Christians and Quistians in the GOP." In *God at the grass roots, 1994: The Christian right in American elections,* ed. Mark J. Rozell and Clyde Wilcox. Lanham, Md.: Rowman & Littlefield.

___. 1997. "Minnesota: Onward ouistant soldiers? Christian conservatives confront their limitations." In *God at the grass roots, 1996: The Christian right in American elections,* ed. Mark J. Rozell and Clyde Wilcox. Lanham, Md.: Rowman & Littlefield.

Goldberg, Carey. 1996a. "In abortion war, high-tech arms." *New York Times,* 9 August.

___. 1996b. "In rockets' red glare, it's party, party, party." *New York Times,* 12 August.

Green, John C., Mark J. Rozell, and Clyde Wilcox. 1995. "Faith, hope, and conflict: The Christian right in state Republican politics." Paper presented at the annual meeting of the American Sociological Association, 19-23 August, Washington, D.C.

Greenhouse, Steven. 1996. "Citing abortion bill veto, union head rejects Clinton." *New York Times,* 30 June.

Grenzke, Janet. 1989. "Shopping at the congressional supermarket: The currency is complex." *American Journal of Political Science* 33:1-24.

Gugliotta, Guy. 1996. "Interest groups' spending had varied success." *Washington Post,* 7 November.

Gugliotta, Guy, and Ira Chinoy. 1997. "Outsiders Made Erie Ballot a National Battle." *Washington Post,* 10 February.

Gugliotta, Guy, and Ruth Marcus. 1997. "Undisclosed donations aided GOP cause in '96." *Washington Post,* 30 October.

Gusmano, Michael. Forthcoming. "The doctors' lobby." In *After the revolution: PACs and lobbies in the new Republican Congress,* ed. Robert Biersack, Paul S. Herrnson, and Clyde Wilcox. New York: Allyn and Bacon.

Guth, James. 1995. "South Carolina: The Christian right wins one." In *God at the grass roots, 1994: The Christian right in American elections,* ed. Mark J. Rozell and Clyde Wilcox. Lanham, Md.: Rowman & Littlefield.

___. 1997. "South Carolina Christian right: Just part of the family now?" In *God at the grass roots, 1996: The Christian right in American elections,* ed. Mark J. Rozell and Clyde Wilcox. Lanham, Md.: Rowman & Littlefield.

Handler, Edward, and John R. Mulkern. 1982. *Business in politics.* Lexington, Mass.: Lexington Books.

Herrnson, Paul S. 1994. "The National Committee for an Effective Congress: Liberalism, partisanship, and electoral innovation." In *Risky business: PAC decisionmaking in congressional elections,* ed. Robert Biersack, Paul S. Herrnson, and Clyde Wilcox. Armonk, N.Y.: M. E. Sharpe.

___. 1997. *Congressional elections: Campaigning at home and in Washington.* Washington, D.C.: CQ Press.

Hertzke, Allen D. 1988. *Representing God in Washington: The role of religious lobbies in the American polity.* Knoxville: University of Tennessee Press.

___. 1993. *Echoes of discontent: Jesse Jackson, Pat Robertson, and the resurgence of populism.* Washington, D.C.: CQ Press.

Howe, Daniel Walker. 1980. "Religion and politics in the antebellum North." In *Religion and American politics,* ed. Mark A. Noll. New York: Oxford University Press.

Hrebenar, Ronald J. 1997. *Interest group politics in America.* 3d ed. Armonk, N.Y.: M. E. Sharpe.

Human Rights Campaign. 1996. "The 104th Congress in perspective." Washington, D.C.: Human Rights Campaign.

"Is the NRA 'overrated'?" 1995. *Campaigns & Elections,* October/November, 49.

Jackson, Brooks. 1990. *Honest graft.* Washington, D.C.: Farragut Publishing Co.

____. 1996a. "Business helps bankroll GOP, Democratic conventions." CNN. Transcript. AllPolitics.com. 6 August.

____. 1996b. "Religious right, convention might." CNN. Transcript. AllPolitics.com. 8 August.

Labaton, Stephen. 1996. "A new arena for ads and political influence." *New York Times,* 13 August.

Ladd, Everett Carll. 1978. *Where have all the voters gone? The fracturing of America's political parties.* New York: Norton.

Lengle, James I., and Byron Shafer. 1976. "Primary rules, political power, and social change." *American Political Science Review* 70: 25–40.

Levick-Segnatelli, Barbara. 1994. "The Washington PAC: One man can make a difference." In *Risky business: PAC decisionmaking in congressional elections,* ed. Robert Biersack, Paul S. Herrnson, and Clyde Wilcox. Armonk, N.Y.: M. E. Sharpe.

Lovenduski, Joni. 1997. "Gender politics." In *Britain votes,* ed. Pippa Norris and Neil Gavin. Oxford: Oxford University Press.

Maisel, Sandy. 1996. "The platform-writing process: Candidate-centered platforms in 1992." In *Understanding presidential elections: Trends and developments,* ed. Robert Y. Shapiro. New York: Academy of Political Science.

Marcus, Ruth. 1997a. "GOP's issue conferences coincided with Hill action." *The Washington Post,* 24 July.

____. 1997b. "RNC steered funds to outside groups." *Washington Post,* 23 October.

____. 1997c. "Staying ahead of the PACs." *Washington Post,* 25 November.

Master calendar of events. 1996. Republican National Convention.

McBurnett, Michael, Christopher Kenny, and David J. Bordua. 1996. "The impact of political interests in the 1994 elections: The role of the National Rifle Association." Paper presented at the annual meeting of the Midwest Political Science Association, Chicago.

Moss, Jennings. 1994. "Promises, promises: A Clinton report card at the one year mark." *Washington Times,* 20 January.

Mundo, Phillip. Forthcoming. "League of Conservation Voters." In *After the revolution: PACs and lobbies in the new Republican Congress,* ed. Robert Biersack, Paul S. Herrnson, and Clyde Wilcox. New York: Allyn and Bacon.

Mutch, Robert. 1994. "AT&T PAC: A pragmatic giant." In *Risky business: PAC decisionmaking in congressional elections,* ed. Robert Biersack, Paul S. Herrnson, and Clyde Wilcox. Armonk, N.Y.: M. E. Sharpe.

____. Forthcoming. "AT&T PAC: The perils of pragmatism." In *After the revolution: PACs and lobbies in the new Republican Congress,* ed. Robert Biersack, Paul S. Herrnson, and Clyde Wilcox. New York: Allyn and Bacon.

National Association of Realtors (NAR). 1991. *Getting there: How to become a Realtor public official.* Washington, D.C.: NAR.

National Committee to Preserve Social Security and Medicare (NCPSSM). 1996. *104th Congressional scorecard.* Washington, D.C.: NCPSSM.

National Rifle Association (NRA). 1994. *The politics of crime: Winning strategies for your campaign.* Fairfax, Va.: NRA. Multimedia package.

National Women's Political Caucus (NWPC). 1997a. *Campaigning to win: The NWPC guide to running a winning campaign.* Washington, D.C.: NWPC.

____. 1997b. *Candidate recruitment guide for state and local caucus leaders (NWPC).* Washington, D.C.: NWPC.

Nelson, Candice. 1994. "BIPAC: Trying to lead in an uncertain political climate." In *Risky business: PAC decisionmaking in congressional elections,* ed. Robert Biersack, Paul S. Herrnson, and Clyde Wilcox. Armonk, N.Y.: M. E. Sharpe.

Nelson, Candice, and Robert Biersack. Forthcoming. "BIPAC: Working to keep a pro-business Congress." In *After the revolution: PACs and lobbies in the new Republican Congress,* ed. Robert Biersack, Paul S. Herrnson, and Clyde Wilcox. New York: Allyn and Bacon.

Norrander, Barbara. 1992. *Super Tuesday: Regional politics and presidential primaries.* Lexington: University Press of Kentucky.

O'Leary, Brad. 1995. "Fire power: Surprising poll results and election returns show that the National Rifle Association had a lot more to do with November 8 than most pundits realize." *Campaigns & Elections,* December/January, 32.

Ornstein, Norman J., et al. 1997. *New campaign finance reform proposals for the 105th Congress.* Brookings Institution. http://www.brookings.edu/gs/newcfr/reform.htm.

Patterson, Samuel C., and Keith R. Eakins. 1998. "Congress and gun control." In *The changing politics of gun control,* ed. John Bruce and Clyde Wilcox. Lanham, Md.: Rowman & Littlefield.

People for the American Way. 1996. *The politics of distortion: The Christian Coalition's voter guides.* People for the American Way. 31 October. http://www.pfaw.org/ccvoter.htm.

Pew Research Center for the People and the Press. 1997. *Politics, morality, entitlements sap confidence.* Washington, D.C.: Pew Research Center for the People and the Press.

Polsby, Nelson. 1983. *Consequences of party reform.* New York: Oxford University Press.

Pomper, Gerald, with Susan Lederman. 1980. *Elections in America.* New York: Longman.

Potter, John. 1997. "Where are we now? The current state of campaign finance law." In *Abridged campaign finance reform: A sourcebook,* ed. Anthony J. Corrado et al. Brookings Institution. http://www.brookings.org/GS/newcfr/sourceBk.htm.

Republicans for Choice. 1996. *On the 1996 GOP platform committee hearings and the Republican National Convention.* Alexandria, Va.: Republicans for Choice.

Rimmerman, Craig. 1994. "When women run against women: Double standards and vitriol in the New York primary." In *The year of the woman,* ed. Elizabeth Cook, Sue Thomas, and Clyde Wilcox. Boulder, Colo.: Westview.

_____. Forthcoming. "The Gay and Lesbian Victory Fund comes of age." In *After the revolution: PACs and lobbies in the new Republican Congress,* ed. Robert Biersack, Paul S. Herrnson, and Clyde Wilcox. New York: Allyn and Bacon.

Rosenstone, Steven J., and John Mark Hansen. 1993. *Mobilization, participation, and democracy in America.* New York: Macmillan.

Rossotti, Jack E. 1994. "How the little people choose: PAC decisionmaking in the PHH Group, Inc., and the National Air Traffic Controllers' Association." In *Risky business: PAC decisionmaking in congressional elections,* ed. Robert Biersack, Paul S. Herrnson, and Clyde Wilcox. Armonk, N.Y.: M. E. Sharpe.

Rozell, Mark J. Forthcoming. "The WISH List: Moderate women in the GOP Congress." In *After the revolution: PACs and lobbies in the new Republican Congress,* ed. Robert Biersack, Paul S. Herrnson, and Clyde Wilcox. New York: Allyn and Bacon.

Rozell, Mark J., and Clyde Wilcox. 1995. *God at the grass roots: The Christian right in the 1994 elections.* Lanham, Md.: Rowman & Littlefield.

_____. 1996. *Second Coming: The new Christian right in Virginia politics.* Baltimore: The Johns Hopkins University Press.

_____. 1997. *God at the grass roots, 1996: The Christian right in American elections.* Lanham, Md.: Rowman & Littlefield.

Sabato, Larry J. 1984. *PAC power.* New York: Norton.

Sack, Kevin. 1996a. "Differences aside, labor embraces the Democrats." *New York Times,* 26 August.

_____. 1996b. "Organized labor fires back on Medicare." *New York Times,* 30 August.

Schlozman, Kay Lehman, and John T. Tierney. 1986. *Organized interests and American democracy.* New York: Harper and Row.

Shaiko, Ron, and Marc A. Wallace. Forthcoming. "From Wall Street to Main Street: The National Federation of Independent Businesses and the Republican majority." In *After the revolution: PACs and lobbies in the new Republican Congress,* ed. Robert Biersack, Paul S. Herrnson, and Clyde Wilcox. New York: Allyn and Bacon.

Shields, Mark. 1997. "Seduced, abandoned and bewildered." *Washington Post,* 20 October.

Sinclair, Barbara. 1997. *Unorthodox lawmaking: New legislative processes in the U.S. Congress.* Washington, D.C.: CQ Press.

Sorauf, Frank. 1984. *What price PACs?* New York: Twentieth Century Fund.

———. 1988. *Money in American elections.* San Francisco: Scott Foresman.

Stern, Philip. 1988. *The best Congress money can buy.* New York: Pantheon.

Stone, Peter H. 1997. "GOP jousts with Business Roundtable." *National Journal,* 11 January, 75.

Stronks, Julia. 1994. "The American Association of Publishers PAC." In *Risky business: PAC decisionmaking in congressional elections,* ed. Robert Biersack, Paul S. Herrnson, and Clyde Wilcox. Armonk, N.Y.: M. E. Sharpe.

Swierenga, Robert P. 1980. "Ethnoreligious political behavior in the mid-nineteenth century: Voting, values, cultures." In *Religion and American politics,* ed. Mark A. Noll. New York: Oxford University Press.

Terry, Don. 1996. "Chicago protesters get time slots." *New York Times,* 3 August.

Thomas, Sue. Forthcoming. "NARAL PAC: Battling for women's reproductive rights." In *After the revolution: PACs and lobbies in the new Republican Congress,* ed. Robert Biersack, Paul S. Herrnson, and Clyde Wilcox. New York: Allyn and Bacon.

Tollerson, Ernest. 1996. "Hired hands carrying democracy's petitions." *New York Times,* 9 July.

Toner, Robin. 1997. "Christian Coalition plans to be heard." *New York Times,* 9 June.

Truman, David. 1951. *The governmental process.* New York: Knopf.

Verba, Sidney, Kay Lehman Schlozman, and Henry Brady. 1995. *Voice and equality: Civic voluntarism in American politics.* Cambridge, Mass.: Harvard University Press.

Verhovek, Sam Howe. 1996. "Corporate receptions provide lawmakers with loophole in ethics rules." *New York Times,* 16 August.

Walker, Jack. 1983. "The origins and maintenance of interest groups in America." *American Political Science Review* 77: 390–406.

Wayne, Leslie. 1996. "Like other television shows, convention had sponsors." *New York Times,* 1 September.

Welch, Susan, et al. 1998. *American government.* 6th ed. Belmont, Calif.: West/Wadsworth.

Welch, William P. 1982. "Campaign contributions and legislative voting: Milk money and dairy price supports." *Western Political Quarterly* 35: 478–495.

Wilcox, Clyde. 1988. "I owe it all to me: Candidates' investments in their own campaigns." *American Politics Quarterly* 16: 266–279.

———. 1989. "Organizational variables and contribution behavior of large PACs: A longitudinal analysis." *Political Behavior* 11: 157–173.

———. 1990. "Member to member giving." In *Money, elections, and democracy,* ed. M. Nugent and John Johannes. Boulder, Colo.: Westview.

———. 1992. *God's warriors: The Christian right in twentieth-century America.* Baltimore: The Johns Hopkins University Press.

———. 1994. "Coping with increasing business influence: The AFL-CIO's Committee on Political Education." In *Risky business: PAC decisionmaking in congressional elections,* ed. Robert Biersack, Paul S. Herrnson, and Clyde Wilcox. Armonk, N.Y.: M. E. Sharpe.

Wilson, James Q. 1962. *The amateur democrat: Club politics in three cities.* Chicago: University of Chicago Press.

Wolf, Richard. 1996. "Labor unions are back and packing some power." *USA Today,* 15 October.

Wright, John R. 1985. "PACs, contributions, and roll calls: An organizational perspective." *American Political Science Review* 79: 400–414.

———. 1996. *Interest groups and Congress: Lobbying, contributions, and influence.* Boston, Mass.: Allyn and Bacon.

"The youth vote." 1996. *New York Times,* 22 July.

Index